Eli Manning

Read all of the books in this exciting, action-packed biography series!

Hank Aaron

Muhammad Ali

Lance Armstrong

David Beckham

Barry Bonds

Roberto Clemente

Sasha Cohen

Joe DiMaggio

Tim Duncan

Dale Earnhardt Jr.

Doug Flutie

Lou Gehrig

Wayne Gretzky

Derek Jeter

Sandy Koufax

Michelle Kwan

Eli Manning

Peyton Manning

Mickey Mantle

Jesse Owens

Cal Ripkin Jr.

Alex Rodriguez

Wilma Rudolph

Annika Sorenstam

Ichiro Suzuki

Jim Thorpe

Tiger Woods

SPORTS HEROES AND LEGENDS™

Eli Manning

by Matt Doeden

 Twenty-First Century Books/Minneapolis

Twenty-First Century Books
A division of Lerner Publishing Group, Inc.
241 First Avenue North
Minneapolis, MN 55401 U.S.A.

Website address: www.lernerbooks.com

Cover photograph:
© Ben Liebenberg/NFL Photos/Getty Images

Library of Congress Cataloging-in-Publication Data

Doeden, Matt.
    Eli Manning / by Matt Doeden.
        p.   cm. — (Sports heroes and legends)
    Includes bibliographical references and index.
    ISBN 978–0–7613–4171–0 (lib. bdg. : alk. paper)
    1. Manning, Eli, 1981– —Juvenile literature. 2. Football players—United
    States—Biography—Juvenile literature. I. Title.
    GV939.M289D63 2008
    796.332092—dc22 [B]   2008014980

Manufactured in the United States of America
1 2 3 4 5 6 – BP – 13 12 11 10 09 08

Contents

Senior Send-off

Eli Manning had turned down millions of dollars for this moment. A hot sun beat down on the field of the Cotton Bowl stadium in Dallas, Texas, on January 2, 2004—just a day before Eli's twenty-third birthday. The quarterback, dressed in the red and white of the University of Mississippi (Ole Miss) Rebels, led his teammates onto the field for one of college football's biggest bowl games.

A year earlier, Eli had been forced to make a difficult decision. He could declare himself eligible for the NFL draft, or he could return to Mississippi for his senior season. NFL scouts had agreed that Eli would have been one of the draft's top picks after his junior year, and he would have earned a multimillion-dollar contract. But Eli didn't feel like his work at Ole Miss was done. He wanted to lead the Rebels to a successful season and a major bowl victory. Ole Miss hadn't won a bowl game in January—when all of the major bowls are played—since 1970, when Eli's father, Archie, was the team's quarterback. So Eli had told the NFL to wait. Here in Dallas, he was getting the chance to achieve his goal. His sixteenth-ranked Rebels were set to take on the Oklahoma State (OSU) Cowboys, ranked twenty-first, in the Cotton Bowl.

Eli and his offense set the tone early. Ole Miss head coach David Cutcliffe had so much confidence in his senior quarterback that he let Eli call most of the team's plays at the line of scrimmage, a rarity in college games. Eli rewarded his coach by picking apart the OSU defense on an early drive. After moving the Rebels to OSU's 16-yard line, he took the snap, faked a handoff, and rolled to his right. The defense was closing fast, but Eli was ready. He turned, saw an open receiver downfield, and fired the ball across his body. The pass hit running back Tremaine Turner in stride just as he crossed into the end zone. Touchdown!

The Cowboys responded with a touchdown of their own, then intercepted one of Eli's passes on the last play of the first quarter. The good field position led to another touchdown and a 14–7 OSU lead.

The intercepted pass was the only real mistake Eli would make all day. He and the Ole Miss offense fought back, driving the ball to OSU's 25-yard line. Once again, Eli took the snap and dropped back. This time he saw receiver Mike Espy open in the middle of the field. But an OSU defender was closing quickly. Eli fired a fast, crisp pass that hit Espy in the chest just inside the end zone. The OSU defender tried to jar the ball loose, but Espy held on for the tying score. A field goal late in the first half put Ole Miss in the lead, 17–14.

The Ole Miss offense just kept rolling, extending the lead to 24–14 on a Turner touchdown run. Late in the third quarter, Eli and his offense got the ball way back on their own 3-yard line. The Cowboy defense wanted a quick stop to get back into the game. But instead, Eli led his team on a time-consuming 13-play, 97-yard touchdown drive that included two big pass completions on third-and-long (third down and ten or more yards to go) plays. Eli capped off the drive in an unusual way. Not known as a runner, he ran for a touchdown on a quarterback sneak.

The Cowboys made a furious comeback late in the fourth quarter, scoring two touchdowns to narrow the Rebel lead to 31–28. But that was all they could manage. Eli took a knee on the last play to let the final seconds tick off the clock. His teammates stormed onto the field to celebrate the school's biggest win in more than 30 years. Eli completed 22 of 31 passes in the game for 259 yards and two touchdowns, along with a score on the ground. For his efforts, he was named Offensive Player of the Game.

"To come to the Cotton Bowl and have your last game with all of those guys and get out a win . . . is something I will always remember," Eli said. "It's been a great run."

Chapter One

Following in the Footsteps

Elisha Nelson Manning was born on January 3, 1981, in New Orleans, Louisiana, into a family that loved sports. The youngest son of Archie and Olivia Manning, Eli had two older brothers who would become standout athletes and a father who had been an NFL star for more than a decade.

It was little surprise that all three of Archie's sons would become excellent athletes. In the late 1960s, Archie had been a star football player for Ole Miss. He was the team's starting quarterback for three years, passing for a total of 4,753 yards and 56 touchdowns. His strong arm and ability to use his legs to scramble out of trouble got the attention of NFL scouts.

The New Orleans Saints selected Archie as the second overall pick of the 1971 NFL draft. But despite the excitement of being picked so high, going to New Orleans was no blessing for young Archie. The Saints were one of the league's worst teams.

Archie got plenty of playing time, but the team around him was consistently bad. While Archie excited fans with his individual talent, the team's struggles continued year after year. In Archie's eleven full seasons with the team, the Saints weren't able to muster a winning record even once. (Archie played in only ten of those seasons, missing the entire 1976 season with a shoulder injury.)

Archie finished his career with short stints in Houston and Minnesota before retiring to do commentary on the Saints radio broadcasts. Eli's older brothers, Cooper and Peyton, were old enough to remember their dad as an NFL star. But Eli was only three when Archie retired. He remembers his father's career only through stories and old videos.

❝*When I finally [retired from the NFL], it was an upper instead of a downer. . . . Good-bye, football, hello, rest of my life. And hello, Cooper, Peyton, and Eli, and the football I would enjoy through them. A whole new world.*❞

—ARCHIE MANNING

Eli—seven years younger than Cooper and five years behind Peyton—had a lot of catching up to do. But while he liked to play sports as much as either of his brothers, his personality was very different from theirs. Cooper and Peyton were vocal and fiercely competitive. Eli, meanwhile, was much more reserved.

"I was always kind of the quiet one, the shy one," Eli later said of his role in the family. "Sitting around the dinner table, Cooper kind of ran the conversation. He and Peyton and my dad were the ones who carried the conversation. Mom and I never got to do a whole lot of talking."

❝ Eli was . . . very reluctant to show feelings, for anybody or anything. It was sad at times, but funny too. Somewhere along the way he made a rule that you could only kiss him on Sunday nights. Our family has always been big on hugs and kisses, but Eli wasn't interested. I mean not at all. Then he finally gave in a little and agreed to Sundays. One kiss, that's all. Good night, good-bye, see you at breakfast. ❞

—OLIVIA MANNING

Much of Eli's youth was spent watching his brothers play sports. In fact, he spent so much time watching Cooper and Peyton play football, basketball, baseball, and other sports that he got sick of it. Sometimes he'd ask to stay home just to avoid another day of watching. But before long, Eli was playing in games of his own. Just like his dad and his brothers, he especially liked football. His strong arm and understanding of the game made him a natural fit at quarterback.

 According to his mother, Eli didn't start talking until he was three years old. His first word was "ball."

While he excelled on the football field, Eli struggled in the classroom. In first grade, Eli was having trouble reading. His parents were worried that he might have to be held back to repeat the grade.

"As a child, [not being able to read is] embarrassing and frustrating," he later said. "They call on students to read out loud in class and it's one of those deals where you're praying the whole time that they don't call on you."

Olivia didn't want her youngest son to fall behind. She worked hard with him and also had him tutored. Slowly, Eli started to catch up. He didn't have to repeat the grade, and he would grow into an excellent student. Like his brothers, Eli attended the Isidore Newman private school in New Orleans. Both Peyton and Cooper became football stars there in high school. In 1991, when Eli was ten, he watched his brothers play together on the football team. Peyton was the quarterback, while Cooper was his favorite receiver. They led Newman to the state semifinals.

BULLY BROTHER

Peyton liked to pick on his little brother. He would pin Eli down on the ground and rough him up until Eli could answer trivia questions about football. Because he was so much younger, Eli couldn't hope to outmuscle Peyton. Instead, he went to older Cooper for protection.

Cooper's talent had gotten the attention of college scouts. Naturally, Cooper wanted to follow in his dad's footsteps. He accepted a scholarship to play wide receiver at Ole Miss. But before his college football career ever got off the ground, it came to a quick and scary end. Doctors diagnosed him with spinal stenosis, a narrowing of the spinal column in the neck. Cooper would never play competitive football again. Luckily, neither Peyton nor Eli shared this dangerous condition.

Two years later, it was Peyton's turn to pick a college. Many fans assumed that Peyton would follow his dad and his brother to Ole Miss. But Peyton had other ideas. He picked the University of Tennessee instead. He felt Tennessee's football program was stronger at the time. However, his decision left a lot of Ole Miss fans feeling betrayed and angry. Many fans were just plain hostile. "I hope you get hurt," wrote one Ole Miss supporter. Another claimed, "We always loved your dad, but not after this."

With the athletic success of his brothers at Newman, it was no surprise that Eli would follow in their footsteps. He played basketball and baseball. But he excelled in football.

EASY ELI

Eli is a lot more laid-back than either of his brothers. His friends called him "Easy" for his easygoing attitude. In fact, when he found out he was going to be the starting quarterback at Newman, he didn't even think to mention it to Archie for two days. "That's just how he is," Archie said. "He just plays; he doesn't get caught up in the stuff outside the game."

As a freshman in 1995, he took over as the team's quarterback. In his sophomore year, he really established himself, throwing for 2,340 yards and 24 touchdowns and earning all-state honors. By his junior year (1997), Newman was a force. The team's offense flourished under Eli's leadership, often outscoring opponents so badly that Eli didn't even play in the fourth quarter. The team went 9–1 and advanced to the quarter-finals of the state playoffs. That year Eli completed 142 of 235 passes for 2,547 yards and 26 touchdowns.

Even before his final year at Newman, Eli was already being mentioned as one of the best high school quarterbacks in the nation. His great play was a big part of the reason. The growing fame of his brother Peyton, who had flourished at Tennessee and been the top overall pick of the 1998 NFL draft, didn't hurt either. College coaches were recruiting Eli heavily. Ole Miss, his dad's school, was just one of several schools courting him. Major football programs like Florida State, Louisiana State, Virginia, and Texas were also trying to get him. With his talent and his big name, he had his choice of virtually any school in the nation.

❝ *Here's the thing to remember about Eli. He's smart enough to see Peyton has set a terrific example. He might not accept every facet, but he'll latch on to the good stuff."*

—COOPER MANNING

While Peyton was getting most of the headlines that fall, starting for the Indianapolis Colts as a rookie, Eli was putting together an amazing season of his own. Once again, he led Newman to the state playoffs—this time going undefeated in the regular season. But once again, the team lost in the quarterfinals, finishing with an impressive 11–1 record. Eli made the high school All-America team and was named Player of the Year in Louisiana by *USA Today*. In the end, he finished his high school career with 7,389 passing yards (more than Peyton) and 81 touchdowns.

One of Eli's hobbies is collecting antiques. He and his mom used to shop together when he was young, and it's still something he enjoys.

Everyone was wondering where Eli would attend college the next year. At one point, Eli was leaning toward either Texas or Virginia. For some reason, Ole Miss coach Tommy Tuberville hadn't seemed to try very hard to talk Eli into joining the Rebels. But when Tuberville left Ole Miss after the 1998 season, everything changed. David Cutcliffe took over as the Ole Miss coach. Eli was no stranger to Cutcliffe. He'd been one of Peyton's coaches at Tennessee for four years, and Peyton gave him a lot of credit for helping to turn him into a star quarterback.

"I called Eli the day I got the job," Cutcliffe said. "He and I had talked when I was at Tennessee, and he told me he wasn't going to Tennessee. When I got this job, I told him all bets were off. I think that was the first phone call I made."

Eli's struggle to make a decision was over. He was ready to head to Mississippi.

Chapter Two

Mississippi Rebel

Many experts thought the extra pressure of playing football at a school where his father was a legend would weigh heavily on eighteen-year-old Eli. But Eli didn't see it that way.

"It never bothered me when I was thinking of schools that this is where my father went, or that it'd be too much pressure," he said. "It was so long ago, and the students here might know the name, but they weren't here during the time. . . . So it wasn't anything I thought about, and, once I got here, it wasn't a big issue. It hasn't been a problem for me in any way."

Ole Miss fans were excited to see their new quarterback play. But Cutcliffe was going to make them wait. He redshirted Eli for the 1999 season. To be redshirted means that a player can practice with a team but cannot play in games. It's common for first-year players to be redshirted. They get a chance to learn the system and study the college game. But it doesn't cost them a year of eligibility. They can still play for four years after their redshirt year. So Eli watched from the sidelines as Cutcliffe coached the team to an 8–4 record and a win in the Independence Bowl.

A NUMBER OF HIS OWN

Ole Miss had retired Archie's number 18 jersey after he graduated. But when Eli joined the team, the school offered to bring the number out of retirement to let him wear it. Eli declined the offer. He wore number 10 instead.

The redshirt status allowed Eli to focus on his academics. He was a good student, majoring in business (though he eventually settled on a marketing degree). But all the extra time not focused on football also led to some trouble for Eli. One night, he partied too hard and was arrested for public drunkenness. Eli was embarrassed by his poor judgment and vowed to focus all his energy on school and football.

"I was just glad to be away from my parents," he said. "I was having a great time just being a college student, probably too much fun. And I got caught. I got busted on it. . . . It probably changed my life, that whole situation."

In 2000 Eli was an active member of the team. But he still wasn't a starter. Romaro Miller, a senior, was the team's starting quarterback. Eli got to play in only a few games during the regular season. He completed 16 of 33 passes for 169 yards and no touchdowns. He played mostly in situations where the game's outcome was already decided.

❝ I have seen [Peyton] deal with the pressure of being a college quarterback and the whole process. He has taught me how to read and study film, and I usually talk to him once a week about what brothers talk about. But if I need to ask him a question, I know he understands what I am talking about because he was in the same system. ❞

—ELI MANNING ON DEALING WITH THE TRANSITION TO THE COLLEGE GAME

Ole Miss finished the regular season with a 7–4 record, good enough for an invitation to the Music City Bowl, held in Nashville, Tennessee. There, on a bitterly cold day, the Rebels faced West Virginia University. Eli watched helplessly from the sidelines as Miller and the Rebels struggled. West Virginia was running up the score, dominating Ole Miss in every phase of the game.

With his team trailing 49–16, Cutcliffe decided to give Eli a shot. By all appearances, the game was over. But not to Eli. Early in the fourth quarter, he connected with receiver Jamie Armstrong for a 23-yard touchdown, the first of Eli's college career. Four minutes later, he found Omar Rayford in the end zone for an 18-yard score. Then, with less than seven minutes left, he and fullback Toward Sanford hooked up on a 16-yard pass. After Eli threw a two-point conversion to L.J. Taylor, the score was 49–38. Somehow, shocking just about everyone in the stadium, Eli had gotten his team back into the game! But on the Rebels' next drive, Eli's inexperience showed. He was once again moving the Rebel offense, threatening to further cut the lead. But in his hurry, he threw an interception that sealed the victory for West Virginia. He ended the game 12 of 20 (12 completions in 20 attempts) for 167 yards and 3 touchdowns.

"That [game] helped me a lot," Eli said. "It showed me that I can move this team and I can be a college quarterback. It also showed that to the other players. They have more respect and confidence in me."

Eli also had earned the confidence of his coach. Looking ahead to 2001, Cutcliffe knew that Eli would be his quarterback. "The most important thing [Eli] has done in the year and a half he has been here is he hasn't wasted his time as a practice player," Cutcliffe said. "When you're the backup quarterback, that's what you have to do. I think that's paying dividends, so I don't feel like we have a rookie quarterback out there. He's a lot stronger and quicker than when he got here. He has a good mind for the game."

Excitement grew among Ole Miss fans as the 2001 season approached, despite the fact that the team had lost many of its stars (including Miller and running back Deuce McAllister) to graduation or the NFL. But Eli had been big news since the day he'd committed to the university, and his brief appearance in the Music City Bowl had only heightened expectations.

Even Eli's teammates were excited. "[Eli] is not your typical young quarterback," said All-American offensive tackle Terrence Metcalf. "He is very comfortable with the offense and does not shy away from making plays happen. I am very excited about the season and I know that Eli will do a great job."

On September 1, 2001, the Eli Manning era officially began against Murray State. After Murray State opened the scoring with a touchdown, Eli and the Rebels took over. Eli completed pass after pass, picking apart an undermanned Murray State defense. He threw four first-half touchdown passes, including three to receiver Chris Collins. He added a school-record fifth touchdown pass in the second half as Ole Miss cruised to a 49–14 victory. He finished the game completing 20 of 23 passes for 271 yards.

The Rebels' second game, against Auburn University, proved to be much more challenging. Auburn used a powerful running attack to build a 27–0 third-quarter lead. Eli once again tried to lead a late comeback. He took the Rebel offense on three long drives for touchdowns, cutting the Auburn lead to 27–21 with just over four minutes to play. But the Mississippi defense couldn't get him the ball back for one last drive. The game ended with an Ole Miss loss.

❝ *You are going to have good days and bad days. That comes with college football. When you have good days, you play it down and when you have bad games, you have to put it behind you and keep playing. You can't get too high and at the same time you can't get too low.*❞

—ELI MANNING

After bouncing back with road wins at Kentucky and Arkansas State, the Rebels returned home for a big game against rival Alabama Crimson Tide. Alabama was by far the best team Eli and Ole Miss had faced. The Mississippi fans were desperate for a win over the Crimson Tide, which had won the last ten meetings between the teams. But once again, the Rebels found themselves trailing late in the game, 24–14. A touchdown from running back Charles Stackhouse (with a missed extra point) closed the lead to

24–20. After the defense stopped Alabama's next possession, Eli led his offense onto a wet and rainy field for a final drive. With less than two minutes to play, the Rebels needed to move 59 yards for a touchdown. That number became 69 after a holding penalty on the first play. But Eli was calm. He searched the field and found Armstrong for 24 yards. Two plays later, he connected with Sanford, who was wide open on the sideline. Sanford dashed all the way down to the Alabama 4-yard line.

Less than a minute remained. Once again, Eli took the snap. The Alabama defense was blitzing (sending extra defenders to tackle the quarterback). Eli broke to the outside and looked like he was ready to run the ball in. But as the defense closed in, Eli saw running back Joe Gunn open on the 5-yard line. The Ole Miss crowd erupted as Gunn caught Eli's pass and barreled through two defenders to give the Rebels the lead. The Rebels had done it! They'd finally beaten Alabama. "Coach Cutcliffe told me before the winning touchdown that this is the position a quarterback wants to be in at the end of each game," Eli said. "You're the one that decides if your team wins or loses. You're in control."

After a 45–17 win over Middle Tennessee State, Eli and his team had a 5–1 record. Next up was a tough road game against the Louisiana State (LSU) Tigers. The Tigers were another big rival of Ole Miss. Beating them in their own stadium would be a huge victory for Eli and his teammates. LSU controlled the game early, but Eli led the Rebels to two touchdowns in the final two minutes, 25 seconds of the first half. Still, the Tigers held a 24–21 lead after three quarters. Late in the fourth quarter, a blocked punt gave the Rebels great field position. Eli capitalized on it with a 17-yard touchdown pass to tight end Doug Zeigler for a 28–24 lead. A few minutes later, Mississippi sealed the win. With the ball at LSU's 4-yard line, Eli found himself under heavy pressure. Instead of taking the sack, he heaved the ball toward Zeigler, who was in the corner of the end zone. Zeigler jumped over his defender to catch the ball and give his team a big 35–24 victory.

Eli later admitted that he'd gotten lucky on the final touchdown. "I was just trying to throw the ball away," he said. "Luckily, Doug made a great catch for a touchdown."

With the win, Ole Miss improved its record to 6–1. Excitement about the team was about as high as it had ever been. Fans wondered if the team might be able to win the Southeastern Conference (SEC) Western Division and get into one of the major bowl games.

The buzz around the team only grew as the November 3 home game against the Arkansas Razorbacks approached. Early on, the game didn't seem to be anything special. The teams were tied at 10 after three quarters. Each team added a touchdown in the fourth quarter to send the game into overtime. In the college overtime system, each team gets the ball at the opposing 25-yard line. As soon as one team is ahead after equal possessions, the game is over.

Arkansas opened the scoring in overtime with a touchdown. But Eli and the Rebels answered with an 11-yard touchdown pass from Eli to receiver Jason Armstead. After that, the overtimes kept piling up. Neither team scored in the second overtime, then both scored in the third. (After the first two overtimes, teams must go for a two-point conversion instead of an extra point after a touchdown, but both teams' attempts missed.) They traded touchdowns again in the fourth and fifth overtimes.

The game kept going. In the sixth overtime, Eli hit Zeigler for a 15-yard touchdown, then threw to Stackhouse for the two-point conversion and a 50–42 lead. But once again, Arkansas answered with a touchdown and conversion of its own.

Eli broke his own school record with six touchdown passes against Arkansas. Five of the six touchdowns came in overtime.

Tied at 50–50, the game went into a record seventh overtime. Arkansas put the pressure on, pushing the score to 58–50. Once again, Eli and the offense needed a touchdown and a two-point conversion to force an eighth overtime. The home crowd erupted as Eli connected with Armstead for yet another touchdown. Then, on the two-point try, Eli looked to his tight end, Zeigler. Zeigler caught Eli's pass but was tackled just short of the goal line. The two-point try had failed, and Arkansas had won college football's longest game, 58–56.

It was a tough loss for the Rebels, and it sent their season into a tailspin. The team lost its next two games against Georgia and Mississippi State before beating Vanderbilt in the final game of the season. Despite a promising start, the team had finished at a moderate 7–4 and didn't earn an invitation to any bowl games. It was a bitterly disappointing finish.

Eli was named to the 2001 Verizon Academic All-America second team. The team honors excellence both on the field and in the classroom.

The team hadn't accomplished what it hoped to, but individually, Eli had enjoyed a great season. He completed 259 of 408 passes for 2,948 yards and 31 touchdowns. Better still, he threw just 9 interceptions. For most Mississippi fans, those numbers were plenty of reason for optimism. And with a new girlfriend, fellow student Abby McGrew, Eli had reason for optimism in his personal life as well.

Chapter | Three

Up-and-Down Season

Entering the 2002 season, fans had high hopes for Eli and the Rebels. Before the team even took the field, many experts were talking about Eli as a possible Heisman Trophy candidate. (The Heisman goes to the best player in college football, chosen by sports journalists and past Heisman winners.)

Everything started out according to plan. The Rebels easily beat an undermanned Louisiana-Monroe team 31–3, then dispatched Memphis 38–16 to move to 2–0. Yet Eli wasn't particularly impressive in either game. Their first real test came September 14 against the Texas Tech Red Raiders. Texas Tech jumped out early with a 28–7 halftime lead. Ole Miss looked terrible on defense, special teams, and even on offense. Eli improved in the second half, pulling Ole Miss to within a touchdown midway through the fourth quarter. That was as close as they'd get, though. Texas handed the Rebels their first loss of the season, 42–28. Eli's passing performance (going 34 of 57 for 374 yards), however, gave fans some hope that the team could bounce back.

Vanderbilt was up next, and the Rebels were heavily favored. But once again, the Mississippi defense played poorly. After building a 38–17 lead by the fourth quarter, Ole Miss watched Vanderbilt storm back to tie the game with less than seven minutes to play.

Eli and the offense took possession of the ball at their own 20-yard line. All the momentum was going Vanderbilt's way. But Eli calmly led his team on an 80-yard touchdown drive, capped by a 23-yard run by Ronald McClendon. The Rebels escaped with a 45–38 win. But it had been a lot closer than it should have been.

How would the team recover from such mediocre play? Their next game was against the Florida Gators, always one of the top teams in the nation. Even Eli and his teammates knew that most people would be expecting Florida to win the game. "This is a big game," Eli said. "Since I've been here, [Florida is] probably the best team I've faced so far. It's going to be a challenge for us."

The game featured two of the SEC's best quarterbacks, Eli and Rex Grossman. Many experts predicted an offensive shoot-out. But the game didn't start out that way—especially for the

Rebels. Florida took a 14–2 lead into halftime, with Mississippi's only points coming off a safety (two points given to the defense for tackling a player in his own end zone). But Grossman fell apart in the second half. He threw an interception to Matt Grier early in the third quarter, and Eli and the offense quickly drove the ball for a touchdown and a two-point conversion. A few minutes later, Grier intercepted Grossman again, this time returning it himself for a score. With the extra point, Ole Miss had a 17–14 lead. Neither offense could make anything happen for the rest of the game, and the Rebels walked away with a shocking victory. Even more surprising was that they'd won despite a bad game from Eli. He'd gone just 18 of 33 for 154 yards, and for the first time in his college career, he didn't throw a touchdown pass. Nevertheless, the Ole Miss fans stormed the field to celebrate the rare victory over the Gators with the team. Suddenly, Ole Miss was looking like an SEC contender once again.

The Rebels kept going the next week with a 52–17 win over Arkansas State. The Rebels were 5–1, ranked twenty-first in the nation, and headed into a critical game at twenty-fourth-ranked Alabama. But their run of success came to a screeching halt against the Crimson Tide. Alabama jumped out to a 14–0 lead and never looked back. Eli was under fire all day as Alabama's defensive linemen recorded sack after sack. He and the offense were never able to gain any momentum, while the Crimson Tide scored repeatedly. When the final seconds finally ticked off, the Rebels walked off the field having lost 42–7.

---

66 *Sometimes you have tough seasons or tough games. . . . I thought I played as smart as I could, but things got frustrating at times.* 99

—ELI ON OLE MISS'S 2002 SEASON

The season only got worse from there. The team got blown out again the next week, 48–28, at Arkansas. Then they lost at home to Auburn, 31–24. The losing streak grew to five games with road losses to Georgia and LSU. In the span of a month, the team had gone from SEC-title contender to a team fighting for a shot at a bowl game.

Likewise, Eli had gone from being a Heisman front-runner to having no shot at all at the award. A 24–12 win over Mississippi State in the last game of the regular season lifted the team's record to 6–6, just barely good enough to qualify for a bowl game. They were set to play Nebraska in the Independence Bowl.

The Rebels' late-season collapse was only one of the stories that Ole Miss fans were talking about, however. Eli was winding up his junior season. Many NFL experts said he'd be a high draft pick if he chose to skip his senior season and go pro. But Eli didn't want to think about his next step yet. "I don't know [what I'll do]," Eli said. "I'm going to have to look at it after the bowl game."

Eli didn't tell anyone—even his dad—whether he was planning to go pro or return to Ole Miss after his junior year. "I'm kind of a guy that [will] take all the information in, but then sit down and decide [for] myself," he later said. "I don't like people knowing what I'm thinking."

On December 27, the Rebels took on the Nebraska Cornhuskers in the Independence Bowl. Nebraska had come into the season as one of the top teams in the nation but had struggled to a 7–6 record. Like Ole Miss, the Cornhuskers were struggling to finish the season with a winning record. The Independence Bowl wasn't one of the season's most glamorous bowls, but Eli was determined to win it.

Early on, Nebraska was in command. They built a 10–0 second-quarter lead and were putting heavy pressure on Eli. Eli later admitted his offense had taken a while to find its rhythm.

"But we came out fighting. Eventually, we got a handle on their blitzes and pressure," he told reporters.

College bowls are different from a playoff system. A few NCAA conferences always send their conference champs to certain bowl games (unless those teams qualify for the national championship game). But most of the bowl organizations choose which teams to invite. They select teams depending on rankings, recent bowl matchups, and several other factors. Because of the many factors involved, a moderate record of 6–6 can earn a team a trip to a bowl game even though a 7–4 record the previous year did not.

Ole Miss stormed back late in the half. Eli connected with receiver Kerry Johnson to put the Rebels on the board. Then, with less than two minutes to play in the half, his 42-yard pass to Mike Espy set up a touchdown run by Sanford. The Rebels took their first lead late in the third quarter on another Sanford touchdown, and the defense did the rest. As the final whistle sounded, Eli, his teammates, and their fans celebrated a 27–23 victory.

But would it be Eli's last game in a Mississippi uniform? Eli needed to choose between declaring himself eligible for the NFL draft or playing his senior year at Ole Miss. Peyton had faced the same decision after his junior season at Tennessee, and he'd decided to return for one more year of school. Would Eli risk injury by returning for another year of college ball? Many fans expected that he was ready to join his brother in the NFL.

Eli called a press conference to let the world know his decision. In his typical style of few words, he announced that he was going to stay at Ole Miss for another year. "It just came down to, 'Do you want to go? Or do you want to stay?' And I wanted to stay."

Chapter Four

Senior Season

From the moment Eli announced that he was returning for his senior season, Ole Miss fans were talking about his Heisman Trophy chances. He had a lot of what it takes to win the award. He was an offensive player who put up big numbers. He had plenty of name recognition—after all, his brother was already breaking records in the NFL. The only big part of the Heisman picture that remained uncertain was the quality of his team. The award almost always goes to a player from one of the top teams in the nation. Six or seven wins for Ole Miss, as in previous years, wouldn't be enough. Eli would have to lead his team to more success to have a shot at college football's most prestigious award.

But one person at Ole Miss didn't seem concerned about the award—Eli himself. He had never liked to promote himself, and he asked the school not to campaign for him. (Many universities make a big deal out of having a Heisman hopeful, putting

up billboards and posters, making special T-shirts, and organiz-
ing special promotions.)

---

66 *If I'm a Heisman Trophy candidate late this season,
great. It means we're winning games.* 99

—ELI, EARLY IN HIS SENIOR YEAR

Fans, players, and coaches had plenty of reasons to be
optimistic as Eli and his team prepared for the 2003 season.
"Anytime you have a veteran quarterback coming back with
that type of ability, it is certainly a good feeling," Cutcliffe said of
his team's prospects.

The Rebels opened their season on the road against
Vanderbilt. It was a game that many experts expected Ole Miss to
win easily. But the team wasn't sharp, and they needed a 54-yard
field goal from kicker Jonathan Nichols to pull out a 24–21 win.

Game two was also on the road, this time against the
Memphis Tigers. Once again, it was a game Eli and his teammates were favored to win. And again, they came out flat,
quickly falling behind 14–0. The early deficit seemed to spark Eli
and the offense, though. Eli looked sharp as he led the team to
scores on six consecutive possessions. When Eli and receiver
Bill Flowers hooked up for a 40-yard touchdown pass—Eli's

fourth of the day—the Rebels held a 34–21 lead. The team finally seemed to be living up to expectations.

But it all came crashing down in a disastrous fourth quarter. The defense gave up one big play after another, including a 92-yard touchdown pass. And Eli didn't help either, throwing two critical interceptions. By the time it was over, a shocked Rebel team was walking off the field with a 44–34 loss.

Eli and his teammates were disappointed. But they did their job the next week, easily beating Louisiana-Monroe 59–14. The next real test came in the season's fourth game, against Texas Tech. Eli had been waiting more than a year for the game. He hadn't played well against the Red Raiders the year before, and he was eager to atone for the poor performance.

Fans came to the stadium expecting an offensive shoot-out, and they weren't disappointed in that regard. Both offenses marched up and down the field, scoring almost at will. Eli played well, throwing for more than 400 yards, but Texas Tech quarterback B.J. Symons matched him throw for throw. The late stages of the game, however, seemed almost like a repeat of the Memphis game. The Rebels had built up a 45–34 lead with about eight minutes to play, but the defense could do nothing to stop a furious Red Raider comeback. Texas Tech scored two late touchdowns to steal the win, 49–45. It was the second time in three games that Ole Miss had blown a lead of 10 or more points in the fourth quarter. Nothing seemed to be going their way. They knew they needed to recover quickly, though. The team was set to face the powerful Gators in Florida the next week.

The Gators were tough at home. They hadn't lost at home to an unranked opponent in fourteen years—a streak of 58 games. So the Gator fans who filled the stadium expected nothing less than another Florida victory. And early on, it looked like they'd get it as Florida jumped out to a 14–3 lead. But Eli and his offense kept working. Florida's pass defense was tough, so the Rebels relied on the running game to climb back into contention. Late in the fourth quarter, the Gators were clinging to a 17–13 lead. After a Florida punt, the Rebels had the ball at midfield. They needed a touchdown. Eli led the drive, completing two big passes to Chris Collins. Running back Vashon Pearson capped the drive with a 1-yard touchdown run for a Rebel 20–17 lead. Florida couldn't answer back, and the Rebels held on for the upset victory. Despite all their early season troubles, they were 2–0 in conference play and starting to regain their confidence.

❞ *I'll tell you this about Eli: He's taken this leadership role seriously. He's been vocal, he's led by example, and done all the things you'd expect a leader to do.* ❟

—DAVID CUTCLIFFE

The big road win seemed to change everything. The Rebels were on a roll, winning a nonconference game against under-manned Arkansas State 55–0. Next up was Alabama. The Crimson Tide had a stifling defense that hadn't allowed a touchdown in six quarters. Eli and his teammates also remembered the 42–7 beating they'd taken at the hands of the Crimson Tide the year before. They were ready for revenge.

Getting it didn't take long. The Rebels' offense exploded in the first quarter. Eli connected with receiver Taye Biddle for touchdown passes of 23 and 55 yards. The offense added a Brandon Jacobs running touchdown and a field goal to take a quick 24–0 lead.

Alabama never recovered. Eli continued to dominate, throwing for his third touchdown and running the ball in for another. A few late scores weren't nearly enough to get Alabama back into the game, and the Rebels walked off 43–28 winners. Better yet, they were 3–0 in the SEC.

"Our start to the game was just outstanding," Cutcliffe said. "There is plenty to build off of in that game and we want to continue to get better. I was real proud of our effort, and [I] think we played real physical."

The winning streak extended to five with home wins over Arkansas (19–7) and South Carolina (43–40). The Rebels were 5–2 overall but 5–0 in the SEC, the conference's only undefeated team. As a result, they were ranked twentieth in the nation. For the first time in decades, the team had a chance to play in a major bowl. With two losses, they had no hope of a national title against teams with better records in other conferences. But an SEC Western Division championship was a very real goal.

The biggest challenge remaining on their schedule appeared to be a road game against Auburn, a team that had entered the season ranked sixth in the nation but had stumbled to a 6–3 record. It was a tight game, with Auburn holding a late 20–17 lead. That was when Eli and the offense took over at their own 20-yard line. They needed a field goal to tie or a touchdown to win. Several times, the Auburn defense seemed to be on the verge of ending the Rebel winning streak. But on a third-and-11 play, Eli completed a 16-yard pass to Bill Flowers. Later, on another third-down play, he saw Lorenzo Townsend streaking down the sideline and heaved a critical 49-yard pass that set up a Brandon Jacobs rushing touchdown. Mississippi's 24–20 lead barely held up when an Auburn receiver dropped what appeared to be an easy touchdown pass with time running out. Ole Miss got their sixth win in a row and moved to 6–0 in the conference.

"This is the reason I came back for my senior year, to lead this team to [the SEC championship game]," said an excited Eli.

The hopes of reaching that title game hinged on the second-to-last regular-season game of the year, at home against the

LSU Tigers. The winner would win the division and play for the SEC title. It wouldn't be easy, though. LSU was the nation's third-ranked team (Mississippi had moved up to 15 in the rankings). The buildup for the game was huge. Tickets were nearly impossible to get. The media pressure was intense, especially on Eli, who by then was considered one of the Heisman front-runners.

The game itself turned out to be a defensive struggle. LSU's stifling defense frustrated Eli and the Rebel offense for most of the game, especially with a relentless pass rush that didn't allow Eli time to find open receivers. In fact, the only points Ole Miss scored in the first three quarters came on an interception return from the defense.

"[LSU has] a good defense and we just couldn't get things going with our receivers," Eli said. "I was trying to do my best. I didn't have my best game. That's just what happens. It's not a lack of work or focus. It's just the way football goes. Some days you're on, some days you're not."

But as badly as the Rebel offense was playing, they still had a shot early in the fourth quarter. Trailing 17–7, they moved the ball downfield. The highlight of the drive came on a third-and-14 play in which Eli completed a 43-yard pass to Flowers. Four plays later, he tossed a touchdown pass to Jacobs to pull the Rebels within 3.

The Ole Miss defense did its part, forcing an LSU punt. Then Eli moved the team into field goal range, but kicker Jonathan Nichols missed a 36-yard attempt that would have tied the game. Again, the Rebel defense forced a punt. With just over two minutes to play, Eli had one last chance. But on a fourth-and-10 play, one of his linemen accidentally stepped on his foot, causing him to slip—a sack. LSU took over possession and held on to the 17–14 victory. Eli's dreams of an SEC title had slipped away.

"We had our opportunities and we just didn't [take] them," he said. "We just couldn't make the plays we needed to. We just, for whatever reason, weren't as sharp as we had to [be] to win the game."

The Rebels bounced back with a 31–0 win over in-state rival Mississippi State in the season's final regular-season game. Eli threw for 260 yards and three touchdowns in the win, which improved the Rebels' record to 9–3 (7–1 in the SEC), good enough for an invitation to the Cotton Bowl in Dallas.

In the second quarter of the Cotton Bowl, Eli eclipsed 10,000 career passing yards. He joined Peyton as one of only five quarterbacks in SEC history to reach that milestone.

On December 13, Eli traveled to New York for the announcement of the Heisman Trophy winner. His poor performance in the LSU game had badly hurt his chances of winning the award, however, and Oklahoma quarterback Jason White earned the honor instead. Pittsburgh wide receiver Larry Fitzgerald finished second in the voting, and Eli finished third. By just missing the Heisman, he seemed to be carrying on a family tradition—Archie finished third in the 1970 voting, while Peyton finished second in 1997.

HIGH HONORS

Eli didn't win the Heisman in 2003, but he got plenty of awards. He won the Johnny Unitas Golden Arm Award as the nation's best senior quarterback. He got the College Hall of Fame Scholar Athlete Award for his efforts in the classroom and on the field. And he was named SEC Player of the Year.

Several weeks later, the disappointment of not winning the Heisman was easily forgotten with the huge win over Oklahoma State in the Cotton Bowl. Eli's two-touchdown performance in the 31–28 Ole Miss victory gave the Rebels their tenth win of the season. The year-end Associated Press poll ranked them 13th in the nation. It was a perfect way for Eli to end his college career.

"It's been a fun ride," Eli said of his years at Ole Miss. The NFL was waiting.

Chapter Five

A Giant Step

Eli's brilliant senior season had only raised his stock among NFL scouts. He had everything an NFL team was looking for. The twenty-three-year-old was big, standing six-foot four. He had a strong arm. He was smart and experienced. Eli traveled to cities around the country, going to workouts for NFL teams.

The 2004 draft was filled with promising quarterbacks. Eli and North Carolina State star Philip Rivers led the way. The San Diego Chargers held the first pick and were expected to take Eli. But Archie and Eli were concerned about the Chargers' organization. San Diego had struggled badly in recent years, and the Mannings questioned the team's ability to win. Archie had spent most of his NFL career with a terrible team, and Eli didn't want to suffer the same fate.

They hired agent Tom Condon to help deal with the situation. Condon called the Chargers' general manager and advised him not to select Eli with the pick. (Condon said that Archie had asked him to do this, but Archie denied making the request.) Reports about the demands soon went public, casting Eli into a negative light with many fans. The Chargers stood firm. They were willing to discuss a trade, but if they held the first pick come draft day, they intended to use it on Eli. In response, Eli said that he'd refuse to play for San Diego. The situation grew uglier and uglier.

Comparisons of Eli to Peyton were inevitable as the NFL draft approached. Many scouts agreed that Eli had a stronger arm than Peyton did but that Peyton's accuracy was superior. They also noticed the difference in the brothers' demeanor. Peyton was enthusiastic and emotional. He was very animated on the field, unafraid to celebrate a big touchdown. Eli, meanwhile, always seemed cool and collected. He never seemed to get too high or too low.

By the time draft day arrived on April 24, the Chargers still held the top pick. They'd been in trade talks with the New York Giants, which had the fourth pick, but nothing had been announced. Eli went to Madison Square Garden in New York

City to learn his fate. The crowd got very quiet as NFL commissioner Paul Tagliabue stepped to the podium to announce the first pick. Then they booed loudly as Tagliabue read Eli's name. Eli was visibly disappointed as he held the Chargers' jersey he was handed on stage (with the fans still loudly booing him). But he refused to put on the San Diego cap he was given. He was prepared to tell reporters that he planned to go back to school to get a law degree instead of playing for the Chargers.

The Giants took Rivers with the fourth pick, still desperately trying to work out a trade for Eli. In the meantime, Charger coach Marty Schottenheimer called Eli and told him that a plane was waiting to bring him to San Diego. But Eli never had to get on that plane. The Giants and Chargers finally agreed on a trade later in the day. The Giants sent Rivers and three other draft picks to San Diego for Eli.

"I was walking between interviews, and a little kid ran into the room and said I had been traded to the Giants," Eli said. "I thought he might be joking with me." It was no joke. After a long, stressful day, Eli had his wish. He was going to play for the New York Giants.

The Giants were just as excited as Eli. "This is a very special football player," Giants head coach Tom Coughlin said. "Obviously, the pedigree is excellent. His performance in the workouts was outstanding, his accuracy, all his throws, how he carried himself with a certain dignity and class. It was a very exciting thing to witness."

❝ Obviously, this was not the ideal situation. It was a decision we felt strongly about, and that's why we . . . told the Chargers what we did. But I didn't dictate this [trade]. I didn't know I would be [in New York].❞

—ELI ON THE DRAFT-DAY TRADE

The move worked out well for Eli's longtime girlfriend, Abby, as well. She was getting into a career in fashion and would eventually get a job designing gowns and wedding dresses for a major designer. New York, a center of fashion, was an ideal destination for her.

The Giants quickly cut ties with their former quarterback, Kerry Collins. They worked with Eli and Condon to sign Eli to a contract. The two sides finally agreed to terms on July 30—the same day Giants training camp opened in Albany, New York. The six-year contract was loaded with incentives (bonuses paid for reaching milestones) and could be worth as much as $54 million. Eli was suddenly a very rich young man.

Eli couldn't wait to get started on his pro career. "I just wanted to get in the car and get [to training camp], so I didn't take much time to reflect on [the contract]," Manning said. "Now I have to earn it."

Eli wanted to keep wearing number 10 with the Giants, but punter Jeff Feagles already had that number. So the two teammates struck a deal. Eli would pay for a Florida vacation for Feagles and his family. In return, Feagles would let the rookie quarterback have the number.

In the off-season, the Giants had signed veteran quarterback Kurt Warner. Coughlin said that the two quarterbacks were competing for the starting job. But most assumed that Warner would begin as the starter, while Eli learned in a backup role, at least for the first part of the year.

Warner started the Giants' first preseason game, against the Chiefs. Eli came into the game in the second quarter. He didn't do anything too exciting, but he took care of the ball and helped the Giants to a 34–24 win. A later preseason game got Eli more attention—but not the kind he wanted. Against the New York Jets, he came into the game in relief of Warner, who had looked bad in a little more than a quarter of play. Eli looked even worse, though. His first pass was intercepted. His second was badly overthrown. Soon after, he was sacked and fumbled the ball. The Jets scooped it up and ran it back for a score. It didn't get any better. Eli looked slow and unprepared on the field. He finished the game completing just 4 of 14 passes, with two interceptions and two sacks.

❝ *I don't think someone can really prepare you for what I'm about to go through. I watched [Peyton's] rookie season, I talked to him as he went through that, and I think it prepares me somewhat, but I think you have to go through it. You have to learn for yourself.* ❞

—ELI, BEFORE HIS FIRST YEAR WITH THE GIANTS,
ON LEARNING TO PLAY IN THE NFL

If Coughlin had any doubts about using Warner as the starter, that performance had probably erased them. And sure enough, Eli was watching from the sidelines when the Giants opened their season on September 12 against the Philadelphia Eagles. The game was a disaster for the Giants, though. The Eagles handled them easily, building up a 31–10 fourth-quarter lead.

With the game out of hand and just over two minutes to play, Coughlin decided to give Eli his first taste of regular-season action. Knowing Eli would be nervous, the Giants called a running play. Eli received the snap and handed it off to running back Tiki Barber. Barber dashed to the right and ran 72 yards for a touchdown. It was meaningless, with the game's outcome already decided, but it was still quite a way to start a career. The New York defense forced a punt, and Eli took the field again. His first two pass attempts fell incomplete. But his third try was a 34-yard completion to Barber. He finished the drive 3–9 for 66 yards. However, many would only remember a rookie mistake. On the last offensive play of the game, Eli was rolling out of the pocket (the area behind his linemen). He was looking for a receiver and not paying much attention to the defensive rush. An Eagle defender slammed hard into him, driving him forcefully into the ground and jarring the ball loose. Running back Ron Dayne recovered the fumble, but the game was over. It was a mistake that, in a close game, could have been costly. Clearly, Eli still had a lot to learn.

Eli barely played in the weeks after the opener. In fact, he didn't take a single snap in the team's next five games. What little time he did see was late in blowout games. Warner was playing well and the Giants were winning games, building up a 5–2 record through the end of October. The team appeared to be headed for the playoffs. But a disastrous November changed all of that. Everything seemed to fall apart. Warner wasn't performing, and the team was struggling. Coughlin decided that it was time to give his twenty-three-year-old quarterback a shot. He announced that Eli would start the Giants' home game against the Atlanta Falcons.

A sellout crowd piled into Giants Stadium on November 21. The fans—and even Eli's fellow players—were excited to see the rookie in action. "You could feel the excitement, the anticipation people had for him, to see what he was going to do, how he was going to be," Barber said. "He's going to be our future."

The crowd was pumped up as Eli took the field. Unfortunately, he played like the rookie he was in the first half, and Atlanta built a 14–0 halftime lead. He came out vastly improved in the second half, however. On New York's first drive, he led the team to Atlanta's 6-yard line. On a second-and-goal play, he dropped back and saw tight end Jeremy Shockey in the end zone. He fired a pass that Shockey caught just as two defenders converged on him. Shockey held on for the first touchdown pass of Eli's career. The crowd was going crazy, both to celebrate Eli's big moment and because the Giants had cut the Falcons' lead to 14–7.

The Giants added a field goal early in the fourth quarter to pull to within 4 points. Eli had one last chance with less than two minutes to play. The New York offense took the ball at their own 26-yard line. Eli moved them into Atlanta territory, but the drive stalled there. Atlanta took over and killed the final few seconds for the victory. Eli finished the game 17–37 for 162 yards, 1 touchdown, and 2 interceptions.

Many of his teammates praised Eli's poise in the game. But Eli wasn't so easy on himself. "It was disappointing that we didn't win," he said. "I made a lot of mistakes. It's a long process."

Eli didn't know how right he was. He remained the starting quarterback, but over the next three games—all losses—he was terrible. Against the Baltimore Ravens in week 14, he had a miserable game, completing just 4 of 18 passes for 27 yards and throwing 2 interceptions before being benched in favor of Warner.

"[Eli] obviously struggled," Coughlin said. "We gave him every opportunity to work his way through it. Obviously, at one point, that was not going to happen. He has to stand up and face the fact that he didn't play well. He will have to face his teammates. I expect him to react to this with the hunger to be an outstanding player in this league."

The criticism in New York was building. The city is known for being demanding—and sometimes impatient—with its athletes. Fans were realizing that Eli wasn't simply a younger version of Peyton. They wondered if the Giants had given up too much to get him.

But things got better from there. The next week, the Giants hosted the powerful Pittsburgh Steelers, a team on an 11-game winning streak. Pittsburgh was known for its tough defense, but

Eli held his own in the game, looking for the first time in his NFL career like he truly belonged on the field. The Giants mixed the pass and the run well to keep the score close. In fact, Eli hit receiver Marcellus Rivers with a 1-yard touchdown pass that gave New York a brief 24–23 lead. But in the end, Pittsburgh was just too good and came back for an exciting 33–30 win.

"I felt we were going to win this game," Eli said. "Coming in, I had a good feeling, a better feeling than we've had. I don't know why, going against one of the best defenses in the league. At the end of the game, I thought we had the momentum, that we were going to get something done."

NFL BREAKDOWN

The NFL is made up of two conferences of sixteen teams, the American Football Conference (AFC) and the National Football Conference (NFC). Each conference has four divisions: North, South, East, and West. In the regular season, teams face opponents from both conferences but play others in their division twice. The playoffs then determine the NFC and AFC champions, who face off in the Super Bowl for the national title.

After another close loss the next week to the Cincinnati Bengals, the Giants were 5–10 and on an eight-game losing streak. The final game of the season, against the NFC East division rival Dallas Cowboys, would be Eli's last chance to get a victory as a starter.

After a defensive battle through three quarters, resulting in a 16–7 Dallas lead, Eli and his offense got on track in the fourth quarter. Eli threw his second touchdown pass of the day, to receiver David Tyree. Three minutes later, he connected with Barber to give the Giants a 21–16 lead.

The Cowboys came back with a long, clock-eating drive of their own, resulting in a touchdown, a two-point conversion, and a 24–21 lead. By the time Eli and his offense got the ball back at their own 34-yard line, less than two minutes remained on the clock. It was time for Eli to shine. On the first play of the drive, he narrowly escaped a sack, finding Barber for a 23-yard completion. Eli and Barber worked together to keep the drive moving. With just 16 seconds left, the Giants had a first down at the Dallas 3-yard line.

The coaches called for a passing play. But when Eli got to the line of scrimmage, he didn't like what he saw. The Cowboy safeties were playing deep. That meant Dallas was expecting New York to pass. After all, if the Giants ran the ball and were tackled before crossing the end zone, the clock would keep ticking. A running play would be a huge risk, but Eli didn't think the Cowboys would be prepared for it. So he called an audible (change of play). He took the snap and handed it off to Barber. The running back darted through the surprised Cowboy defense into the end zone. Touchdown! The losing streak was over! With the extra point, the Giants had a 28–24 win. It had been a long, disappointing season, but it had ended on a great note.

"Obviously things haven't gone the way we wanted them to [this season]," Eli said. "We went through some rough times. To end the season on a win, especially the way we did it with a two-minute drive at the end of the game, will hopefully give us some motivation going into the off-season."

Chapter Six

Playoff Push

After the 2004 season, Warner realized that the Giants had become Eli's team. Not wanting to be a backup, he opted out of his contract with New York and signed with the Arizona Cardinals. Ironically, the two teams—and two quarterbacks—faced off at Giants Stadium in week one of the 2005 regular season.

Eli wasn't brilliant in the game, completing just 10 of 23 passes for 172 yards, 2 touchdowns, and two interceptions. But the rest of the offense and the defense played great, leading the Giants to an easy 42–19 win. The team moved to 2–0 after a 27–10 win over the New Orleans Saints in week two. It was supposed to be a road game for the Giants. But because of Hurricane Katrina, which had struck New Orleans just weeks before, the game was held in Giants Stadium.

Next up for the Giants was a trip to San Diego. Charger fans had not forgiven Eli for the way he'd rejected their team in the 2004 draft. They were eager to let him hear about it. A sell-out crowd filled the stadium. The moment Eli stepped foot on the field, a chorus of boos and taunts rained down from the stands. And the fans didn't stop booing Eli all game—every time he took the field. They shouted crude insults at him. They held up signs that said "Daddy's Little Girl," "Hey, Eli, Nobody Likes You," and much more.

"I got about what I expected," Eli said of the reception. "Hopefully, we can put all this—the Chargers and everything that happened—in the past."

Eli held his own in the game. The Chargers jumped out to an early 21–3 lead, but he led the Giants back. Late in the first half, Eli took the snap from San Diego's 5-yard line. The Chargers blitzed him. Eli saw the blitz coming and lofted a soft touch pass to receiver Plaxico Burress in the corner of the end zone. A moment later, linebacker Ben Leber leveled Eli, drawing a late-hit penalty.

Before the 2005 season, the Giants signed former Pittsburgh wide receiver Plaxico Burress. Burress, a big, athletic receiver, would give Eli a reliable target in the passing game.

The Giants were rolling and cut San Diego's lead to 21–20 by halftime. But the combination of San Diego running back LaDainian Tomlinson and quarterback Drew Brees proved too much for the Giants' defense to handle in the second half, and the Chargers cruised to a 45–23 win, much to the delight of their fans. Eli had a great game, completing 24 of 41 passes for 352 yards and 2 touchdowns. But it wasn't nearly enough.

Eli's good play carried into the next week against the St. Louis Rams. He connected with Burress 10 times in the game—twice for touchdowns—to lead the Giants to an impressive 44–24 victory. In the game, by far Eli's best as a pro, he went 19–35 for 296 yards and threw a career-high 4 touchdown passes.

"Just going into the spring and going into training camp, I thought I had a better feel for things," Eli said after the game. "In the first two games, I didn't move in the pocket and didn't feel comfortable with that. I finally just started working on moving in the pocket, standing in there, and shuffling my feet [so] on all my throws . . . I could be as accurate as I want to. And things finally got to that point where I feel comfortable with what we're doing with our plays."

The win was the start of a hot streak for the Giants, who won three of their next four games to improve their record to 6–2. The playoffs looked likely, and an NFC East title seemed within reach. People were starting to wonder whether the Giants were really this good.

Then the Minnesota Vikings came to town. The 3–5 Vikings had struggled mightily on the road and looked to be easy pickings for the sky-high Giants. But Eli—along with many of his teammates—played terribly in the game. Eli threw a career-high 4 interceptions, including one that Viking safety Darren Sharper returned 92 yards for a touchdown. The only highlight for Eli in the 24–21 loss was a 23-yard touchdown pass to Amani Toomer. It was Eli's tenth game in a row with a touchdown pass, the longest streak active in the league at the time.

The team bounced back the next week against division rival Philadelphia. The Eagles were missing their starting quarterback, Donovan McNabb, because of injury, and receiver Terrell Owens because of a suspension. The Giants took advantage. In the second half, Eli led a 69-yard drive to extend New York's lead to 20–10. Then, later in the fourth quarter, he and Burress sealed the win. Eli dropped back and faked a quick pass, causing Burress's defender to hesitate. The speedy receiver streaked down the field, and Eli lobbed a long pass. Burress pulled it in and sprinted to the end zone for a 61-yard score. The 27–17 win moved the Giants to 7–3 and kept them tied with Dallas for the division lead. And more important, it erased the bad feelings that had come with the loss to Minnesota.

Eli posted a quarterback rating of 130.0 in the win over the Eagles. That is the highest single-game rating of his career. The rating is determined by a complicated formula that takes into account a quarterback's completion percentage, touchdowns, and interceptions. A perfect quarterback rating is 158.3.

The Giants lost the following week, 24–21 to the Seattle Seahawks. That set up an important battle with the Dallas Cowboys in Giants Stadium. The winner would take control of the division. It was especially important for the Giants, who had lost in Dallas earlier in the season. If they lost again, the Cowboys would be all but assured of the division crown.

Eli and the offense didn't play well in the game. Eli threw 2 interceptions and completed just 12 of 31 passes for 152 yards and no touchdowns—breaking his streak of 12 straight games with a touchdown. But the Giants' defense didn't let the chance slip away. They smothered the Cowboy offense, building up a 17–0 lead. The Cowboys' comeback attempt fell short, and the Giants claimed first place.

Eli's poor play continued over the next two weeks. He threw three interceptions against the Eagles and then put up modest numbers against the Kansas City Chiefs. But the Giants' defense and running game stepped up, earning a 26–23 win in overtime over Philadelphia and a 27–17 victory over the Chiefs. The Giants had a chance to clinch the NFC East division title in week 16 but came out flat against the Washington Redskins in a 35–20 loss.

❝ *I didn't play as well as I know I can. I'm going to get better. I know I am. . . . I'm going to work hard, and I'm going to do everything I can do to become a guy who can be a leader of this team, and when things aren't going well, take over and get things going. That's where I want to be next year.* ❞

—ELI ON HIS FIRST FULL SEASON AS A STARTER

The loss meant that heading into the season's final week, the Giants still hadn't even clinched a playoff spot. If they beat the Oakland Raiders, they'd still win the division and go to the playoffs. But if they lost the game and the Vikings won, the Giants could end up out of the playoffs altogether. Eli hadn't been playing well in recent weeks, and it was time for the twenty-four-year-old quarterback to step up.

The 4–11 Raiders didn't have much to play for, and it showed. The Giants opened the scoring with a big play—a

95-yard touchdown run from Barber. In the second quarter, it was Eli's turn for a big play. From the shotgun formation (in which the quarterback stands several yards behind the center), he saw Burress shake his defender as he was running across the field. Eli's pass hit Burress in stride. The receiver did the rest, sprinting to a 78-yard score—the longest touchdown pass in Eli's career. The Raiders put up a good fight in the second half, but the Giant defense was too strong. New York's 30–21 victory gave them the NFC East championship and an 11–5 regular-season mark. Eli was headed to his first playoff game.

 Eli finished the 2005 regular season 294 of 557 for 3,762 yards, 24 touchdowns, and 17 interceptions.

Eli knew that it was not time to celebrate yet. He had watched Peyton enjoy all kinds of regular-season success early in his career, only to struggle badly in the playoffs. He'd seen the criticism that followed even a passer as good as Peyton when he couldn't win in the postseason. "All the regular season does is get you to the playoffs," Eli said. "And now you see what you've really got."

Peyton *(left)*, Eli *(center)*, and Cooper Manning *(right)* attend a ceremony at Ole Miss honoring their father, Archie, in 1986. The school retired Archie's jersey, number 18, at the ceremony.

Eli avoids the defense during a game as a freshman quarterback at Ole Miss in 2000.

Eli poses with the Maxwell Award in 2003. The award is given to the best all-around college football player, as selected by a panel of sports journalists.

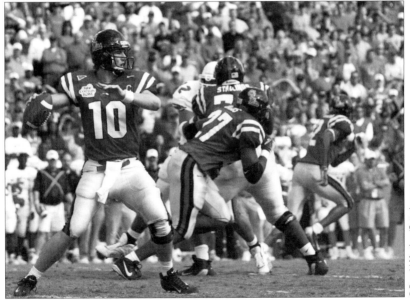

Eli goes back for a pass during the Cotton Bowl in January 2004.

Eli was the first overall pick in the 2004 NFL Draft. Helping him celebrate were his brother Peyton and his wife, Ashley *(first and second from left)*; his mother, Olivia Manning *(third from left)*; his girlfriend (now wife), Abby McGrew *(third from right)*; and his father, Archie Manning.

Eli sets up for a pass during his first professional game as a starter on November 21, 2004.

Eli congratulates his brother Peyton on his victory after the two brothers played their first professional game against each other on September 10, 2006.

The Manning men attend a black tie event in 2007. *From left:* Archie, Peyton, Cooper, and Eli

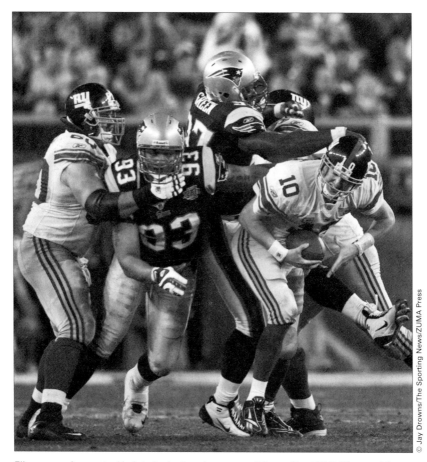

Eli escapes from a tackle late in the fourth quarter of Super Bowl XLII. The resulting pass, caught by David Tyree, set up the game-winning touchdown.

Eli raises the Vince Lombardi Trophy after winning Superbowl XLII on February 3, 2008. The Giants upset the undefeated New England Patriots to win the title.

The division title gave the Giants a home game in the first round of the playoffs. Their opponent, the Carolina Panthers, had relied on the league's fourth-rated defense to build an identical 11–5 mark. The game would be a tough test for Eli and his offense.

The crowd at Giants Stadium was rocking as kickoff approached. They were screaming, cheering, waving towels, and doing all they could to help pump up their team. But it wasn't nearly enough. On the field, the Giants were out-matched—especially Eli and the offense. Carolina's defense pressured Eli relentlessly, driving him into the ground on play after play. The Panthers built a 10–0 halftime lead, and it only got worse for New York in the second half. Eli was way off his game. He was trying to force the ball to receivers who weren't open, and Carolina took advantage with 3 interceptions. Eli also lost a fumble, giving him 4 turnovers in the game. In the end, the Panthers had a convincing 23–0 victory, while Eli and his teammates were left wondering where it had all gone wrong.

"It is shocking because we hadn't really had a performance like this before," Eli said. "We've always found a way to move the ball and score points, but today we couldn't do anything. If I had a reason why, I'd tell you. It's disappointing to end the season this way. . . . Now this is the performance we have to think about for the next months and the off-season."

[The Panthers] were one step ahead of us the whole game. . . . They had an answer for every formation. We ran the ball, they blitzed into it. We threw on play-action and they were dropping back deep. We could never get ahead of them. . . . In a game like this, it's tough to come from behind.

—PLAXICO BURRESS ON THE PLAYOFF LOSS TO THE PANTHERS

Eli's performance in the game was sharply criticized. He completed just 10 of 18 passes for 113 yards. Burress, New York's best receiver, didn't catch a ball. And Eli's 4 turnovers had been very costly. Eli was learning a lesson his brother already knew well: Winning in the playoffs wasn't easy.

Chapter Seven

Growing Pains

The Giants came into the 2006 season with plenty of reason for optimism. The team returned all of its offensive starters from the team that had gone 11–5 the year before. Twenty-five-year-old Eli had another year of experience under his belt. The team had every reason to believe it could defend its NFC East crown and be a force in the playoffs.

Eli was confident that experience would pay off. "This year I know what I want [out of the offense]," he said. "I feel more comfortable taking control of the huddle and correcting someone if they've done something wrong."

The first game of the regular season was a big one, both for the team and for Eli personally. On September 10, the Giants hosted one of the AFC's best teams, the Indianapolis Colts— along with their quarterback, Peyton Manning. It was the first time in NFL history that brothers had quarterbacked opposing teams. The media hyped up the event. They dubbed the game "the Manning Bowl."

"I know [Peyton and Eli] are going to low-key it," Archie said of the boys' approach to playing each other. "They know they're playing a team sport and they've always done that. [Olivia and I are] looking at it that way too, so we don't want too much attention. We're just going to get through it and hope for a whole lot of offense that night."

The Colts jumped out to an early lead, but Eli brought his Giants back. A touchdown pass to Shockey in the third quarter got them within 2 points. With just under five minutes to play in the game, the Colts clung to a 23–21 lead. Eli and the Giants had the ball at their own 10-yard line. Could Eli engineer a dramatic game-winning drive to beat his older brother?

❝ *It kind of hit me . . . when I was out there talking to someone and I see this guy walk by and it was my brother. I found myself watching [Eli] during warm-ups. I was peeking at him during the national anthem. It was kind of neat to be on the same field as him.* ❞
—PEYTON MANNING ON THE MANNING BOWL

The Giants were moving the ball. Eli converted a third-and-2 play with a 19-yard sideline pass to receiver Tim Carter. But as the team was celebrating the big play, they saw an official's yellow flag lying on the ground. The official had called offensive pass interference on Carter, saying he'd pushed defender Nick Harper out of the way. Boos rained down on the stadium as the big video screen showed the replay. It was a questionable call on a game-changing play. An irate Coughlin gave the officials an earful but to no avail. On the next play, Eli tried to force a deep pass over the middle of the field. But Harper intercepted it, all but ending the Giants' hopes. A late field goal gave Indy a 26–21 victory. Eli had played a great game, going 20–34 for 247 yards and 2 touchdowns. But it hadn't been enough to beat his brother.

"I enjoyed watching [Eli] play in person," Peyton said. "He's every bit as good as he looked on TV. He's going to be a great player in this league for a long time. I'm proud to be related to the guy. I'm proud to be his brother."

Eli had a successful—but painful—game the next week in Philadelphia. The Eagles' defense sacked him eight times, but he kept getting back up. Still, Philly held a 24–7 lead entering the fourth quarter, a difficult margin to overcome on the road against a good team. The Giants didn't give up, though. One minute into the quarter, Eli hit Burress with a short pass. The receiver dashed toward the end zone but fumbled the ball as he was running. The ball bounced out from beneath an Eagle defender into the end zone. Luckily, Carter fell on it for the touchdown to close the lead to 10 points. That stroke of luck turned the game around.

The two defenses traded stops on the next several drives. Then, with four minutes to play, Eagle running back Brian Westbrook fumbled the ball. The Giants recovered it for great field position, and Eli capitalized with a 22-yard touchdown pass to Toomer in the back of the end zone. The Giants' defense held the Eagles once more, forcing a Philadelphia punt. Eli and his offense came onto the field with just 58 seconds left in the game. They needed a field goal to tie the game. Eli ran the "hurry-up" offense to perfection, hitting his receivers with quick sideline passes. With 15 seconds left, they were at the Eagle 40-yard line—still too far for kicker Jay Feely to try a field goal. Eli needed to get his kicker closer to the end zone. So he passed once more, this time to Shockey, who stepped out of bounds at the 32-yard line. With the extra yards a kicker needs to set up a field goal, the kick would have extended to about 50 yards. But a personal-foul penalty on the Eagles gave New York an extra 15 yards. The ball was then on the 17-yard line. That made the kick an easy 35-yarder for Feely, and he booted the ball through the uprights. The game was tied 24–24 and headed to overtime!

The Giants won the coin toss and started with the ball. (In the NFL, a coin toss decides who gets the ball first in overtime, and the first team to score wins.) Eli moved the team, but the drive stalled deep in Eagle territory. The ensuing Eagle drive didn't go far, and a punt gave Eli the ball back at the Giants' 15-yard line. He led the offense on a long, steady drive. Eli and Barber worked together to move the Giants slowly down the field. With about three minutes left in the overtime, New York had the ball at the Philadelphia 31-yard line. It was third and 11. Eli needed to get at least a few yards to make the game-winning field goal try for Feely a bit easier. But he got more than a few. The Eagle defense blitzed, hoping to get yet another sack and push the Giants out of field-goal range. Eli saw Burress streaking down the left side of the field and heaved the ball up. The receiver adjusted his route and made the catch in stride. His defender tried to tackle him, but it was too late. Burress was falling into the end zone for the winning touch-down. Eli and his teammates had done it! It was one of the greatest comebacks in team history. It was also Eli's finest game as a pro. He completed 31 of 43 passes for 371 yards and 3 touchdowns in the 30–24 win.

"Some of the plays that [Eli has] been making in close games, he's just showing us that he has something special," Burress said of his young quarterback.

Eli didn't seem quite as special the next week, though, throwing 3 interceptions (as well as 3 touchdowns) in a 42–30 loss to the Seattle Seahawks. But he recovered handily, leading the Giants on a five-game winning streak that pushed their record to 6–2. Eli wasn't putting up huge numbers. But he was managing the game well and allowing the Giants' defense and running game to get the job done.

A rash of injuries hit the Giants around midseason. Burress, left tackle Luke Petitgout, and others missed significant time, and the team—especially the offense—suffered. The slide began with a November 12 loss to the Chicago Bears. In the game, Eli completed just 14 of 32 passes for 121 yards and also threw 2 interceptions. His accuracy continued to suffer the next week against the Jacksonville Jaguars. This 26–10 loss dropped the Giants' record to 6–4.

Eli knew that the Giants' playoff hopes were hanging in the balance. His solution was simple: "Mainly, I've got to start playing better football."

❝ *I don't think we've lost our confidence in [Eli], because we know he's a good player. We just have to make sure that he focuses on those little things and give him a chance by not making it all be on his back.* ❞

—Tiki Barber on Eli's struggles late in 2006

Eli and the Giants seemed to have things back on track in week 12 against the Tennessee Titans, one of the league's worst teams at the time. The Giants' offense scored three first-half touchdowns to take a commanding 21–0 halftime lead. Neither team scored in the third quarter. When New York took possession at their own 29-yard line early in the fourth quarter, they were looking for a drive to put the game away. But instead, on the second play of the drive, Eli made a bad pass that was intercepted by Pacman Jones. Tennessee scored on the ensuing drive to cut the lead to 14 points.

From there, it was a full-blown Giant collapse. Eli and the offense couldn't move the ball or even eat up time. The defense couldn't stop the Titans' offense. Quarterback Vince Young threw his second touchdown pass of the quarter (he'd also run for a touchdown) with less than a minute to play. Shockingly, the Giants had blown a 21-point lead. The game was tied.

The Giants' offense came onto the field with just 44 seconds remaining. If they could get some quick yards, they could still kick a game-winning field goal. Eli opened the drive with a 9-yard pass to Tyree. Then he looked again to Tyree, this time deep. But once again, Jones came away with the ball and ran it back to midfield. "A bad decision on my part," Eli later admitted of his pass attempt.

Three plays later, Tennessee kicker Rob Bironas booted a 49-yard field goal to give the Titans one of the most shocking comeback victories of the year.

Coach Coughlin, like his team, was in disbelief. "I don't have the words to talk about it right now, and I probably won't when I see it [on film]. We're going to be sick about this one forever," Coughlin said.

It was a painful blow for a team that was in the hunt for the playoffs, and the Giants never really recovered. They lost another tight game the next week, 23–20 to Dallas, to drop to 6–6. They exacted a little revenge against Carolina the following week, bouncing back with a 27–13 win. With 3 touchdown passes and no interceptions, it was one of the better games Eli had played in the second half of the season. The win gave New York fans hope. All divisions within the NFC were underperforming. As a result, even at 7–6, the Giants still remained in the playoff race.

The Giants didn't do themselves any favors, though. They lost in week 14 to the Eagles, 36–22. Then they were embarrassed by the Saints, 30–7. Eli completed just 9 of 25 passes in that game for a paltry 74 yards, 55 of those on a touchdown pass to Burress on the fourth play of the game.

"Today was awful," Eli said after the loss to the Saints. "We never had anything quite like this. We've had some tough games and games where we didn't finish well, but today, we didn't do anything."

After the embarrassing loss to New Orleans, the Giant fans were loudly booing their team, individual players (including Eli), and especially the coach. The chant of "Fire Coughlin" rang through the stadium during the second half.

Eli's critics were more vocal than ever. He was blasted in the New York media. The fans seemed to have finally lost patience with him. But somehow, even at 7–8, the Giants still had a shot at the playoffs with one game to go. If they won their final game, against the Redskins, they were almost assured of a spot.

Which Giants team would show up? Would it be the one that had started the season 6–2 or the one who had gone 1–5 since then? A 17-point second quarter answered that question. Tiki Barber, who had announced that he would retire after the season, carried the team to a 34–28 victory. Eli was not spectacular in the game, going just 12–26 for 101 yards, but the Giants didn't need more than that. Barber did it all, rushing for 234 yards and 3 touchdowns. With a record of 8–8, the Giants were headed back to the playoffs. Eli and his teammates would have a chance to redeem themselves and make everyone forget the disastrous end of their regular season.

Tiki Barber

One of the best players Eli ever played alongside was running back Tiki Barber. Barber and his twin brother, Ronde, were born April 7, 1975, in Roanoke, Virginia. Tiki starred at the University of Virginia before the Giants drafted him in the second round of the 1997 draft. Originally, Barber was thought of as a specialty "third-down back" more suited to catching passes than carrying the load on the ground. But once he got the chance to start for the Giants, he never looked back. He broke out in 2000, eclipsing 2,000 all-purpose yards (rushing, receiving, passing, and return yards) in the season. Barber made the NFL's Pro Bowl in 2005, 2006, and 2007. He retired after the 2006 season and took a job with the NBC television network as a broadcaster.

In the first round of the playoffs, the Giants traveled to Philadelphia to face the Eagles. Eli came out looking sharp on the first drive, completing passes of 29, 9, and 15 yards before capping the drive with a bullet pass to Burress in the back of the end zone. The Eagles bounced back to take a 17–10 halftime lead, then extended that lead to 20–10 late in the third quarter. The Giants answered with a field goal early in the fourth quarter to pull to within a touchdown. After a defensive stop, Eli and the offense took over again at their own 20-yard line. Eli moved the team down to the Philadelphia 23-yard line with just seven minutes to play. But then a rash of New York penalties backed the team up. Suddenly, the Giants had a seemingly impossible second and 30 from the Philly 43-yard line. Eli was calm, though. He found Burress on two plays in a row to convert the first down. The Manning-to-Burress combo connected once more on an 11-yard touchdown to tie the game 20–20.

Five minutes remained on the clock, but Eli would never get another chance. The Eagles took the ball and slowly drove down the field, winding down the clock as they went. Eli could only watch helplessly as kicker David Akers scored the winning 38-yard field goal on the game's final play. Despite the fourth-quarter comeback, Eli and his teammates were playoff losers once again.

Eli's season was over. All he could do was get ready for 2007—and root for his brother. Peyton's Colts were having a great postseason. With a thrilling comeback over the New England Patriots in the AFC Championship, Indy was headed to the Super Bowl to face the Chicago Bears, the NFC champs.

> ❝ *I like Eli Manning. I think he is the real deal and he's going to be a top quarterback. . . . [But] right now, it looks like his confidence level isn't up, he's not reading and getting the ball out of there quickly, his decisions aren't really sharp.*❞
> —BROADCASTER AND FORMER NFL COACH JOHN MADDEN

Eli cheered on his brother as the Colts easily handled the Bears for a 29–17 victory in the Super Bowl. Peyton was named the game's MVP. As Eli watched his brother celebrate, he must have wondered if he would ever be in that position.

Chapter | Eight

Highs and Lows

The highlight of 2007 for Eli didn't have anything to do with football. In March, he asked Abby to marry him. She said yes, and the couple began planning a 2008 wedding.

"It's exciting," Eli said. "We've been together for a long time. We're taking the next step, and it's an exciting time in both our lives."

With Barber retired, the Giants' prospects for 2007 were uncertain at best. Eli had yet to establish himself as a consistent, reliable NFL quarterback. The Giants' defense was getting older, and before the season, star defensive end Michael Strahan even considered retirement (but eventually stayed on the team). Many fans and experts saw 2007 as a make-or-break season for Eli. The twenty-six-year-old could no longer be considered a young player. He was becoming an NFL veteran, and it was time for him to show that he belonged. Questions about both his talent and his leadership had surfaced, most notably from former teammate Barber, who had criticized Eli's unemotional style of leading the offense.

The season didn't start out the way New York fans hoped. The Giants opened with an offensive shoot-out against the Cowboys. Neither defense seemed able to stop the opposing offense. Eli was as sharp as he'd ever been. On the opening drive, he and Burress connected on a 60-yard touchdown. It was one of Eli's best games statistically. He went 28–41 for 312 yards and 4 touchdowns (three of them to Burress). But Dallas quarterback Tony Romo was just a bit better, and Dallas earned a 45–35 victory.

Eli bruised his throwing shoulder late in the week one Dallas loss and had to watch the end of the fourth quarter from the sidelines. The injury would continue to hamper him for several weeks.

The Giants fell to 0–2 on the season with a week two loss to the Green Bay Packers, 35–13. Then the defense started playing better and the team was on fire. A 24–17 victory at Washington was the beginning of a six-game winning streak.

Eli didn't play particularly well during the streak. In fact, he had almost as many interceptions (7) as he did touchdown passes (8), and his accuracy was far too low. But a smothering defense and a hot running game, led by backs Derrick Ward and Brandon Jacobs, got the job done.

The winning streak set up a rematch with Dallas, which had jumped out to lead the NFC East. If the Giants hoped to compete with the Cowboys for the division, they badly needed to beat them. But once again, New York's defense couldn't stop Romo, and Dallas pulled away late to win 31–20.

The Giants rebounded with a road win against the Detroit Lions. In one of his better games of the season, Eli completed 28 of 39 passes for 283 yards. More important, he didn't turn the ball over. He was learning that his defense was good enough to win games as long as he didn't hurt the team with costly turnovers.

On November 25, the Vikings came to Giants Stadium. It was a chance for Eli to get a little revenge for one of the worst games of his career two years before, when the Vikings had intercepted him a career-high four times. And Eli had another reason to want to do well. Peyton was in the crowd.

In the first quarter, tied at 7–7, Eli tried to throw a pass over the middle to Shockey. But for some reason, the two weren't on the same page about the tight end's route. Shockey cut one way while Eli threw it the other. Safety Darren Sharper intercepted the pass and dashed 20 yards into the end zone for a touchdown. The Vikings continued to pressure Eli in the second quarter. Safety Dwight Smith picked off another of Eli's passes and returned it to the New York 8-yard line, setting up another Viking touchdown. Largely because of Eli's sloppy play, the Giants found themselves trailing 24–7 at halftime.

Things only got worse in the second half. Early in the fourth quarter, Eli and the Giants had the ball. They were behind by 17 points, but they weren't out of the game yet. Eli led a drive down to the Minnesota 11-yard line. Then lightning struck once again. Eli dropped back and tried to throw the ball to Shockey over the middle. But one of the Viking defenders got a hand on the ball, tipping it up into the air. The ball dropped into the hands of Smith, who returned it 93 yards for a Viking touchdown. And as if that weren't enough, on Eli's next drive, he badly underthrew to a receiver. Viking linebacker Chad Greenway stepped into the passing lane, grabbed Minnesota's fourth interception of the day, and rumbled into the end zone for yet another Viking touchdown. Their 3 touchdowns on interception returns were one short of an NFL record. The game ended with an embarrassing 41–17 loss for the Giants. Eli had thrown 4 interceptions for the second time in his career, both times against the Vikings.

❝ *I did not, in my worst moment, ever think I would be standing here talking about history repeating itself. But it did.***❞**

—TOM COUGHLIN ON ELI'S SECOND
FOUR-INTERCEPTION GAME AGAINST THE VIKINGS

"It wasn't good," Eli said. "When you throw four interceptions, it is never a good day. They took advantage of it and scored on three of them. Every one has its own story. One of them was a tipped ball at the line of scrimmage where I was throwing to Shockey for a touchdown. That is just the way things go sometimes."

It was a new low point in Eli's career. The fan reaction was harsh. Many of the fans were fed up with Eli. They wanted him traded or benched. He didn't seem to be improving, they said. If anything, he seemed to be getting worse. He wasn't making big plays or even taking care of the ball. Others claimed that his quiet, laid-back approach was all wrong for the quarterback position. They said that a quarterback needed to be a team's vocal leader and that Eli simply didn't show enough emotion—for good or bad—on the field. Even Coughlin admitted that he had been thinking about benching his quarterback during the Minnesota game. If 2007 was truly to be the turning point in Eli's career, he seemed to be taking a decidedly wrong turn.

Out of Character

Eli's teammates know he's laid-back by nature. But in a 2006 preseason game, something got under his skin. Receiver Plaxico Burress reported that the normally reserved quarterback was screaming at the other players. "You kind of want to see that from your quarterback a little bit, because it kind of gets everybody else riled up," Burress said. "You say, 'Okay, let's go play. Let's go make some plays for the guy.'"

"Manning has had his moments of superb play," wrote national NFL columnist Don Banks. "But the highlights have been too few and far between, and the struggles too frequent to consider Manning an NFL success story at this point in his career. . . . Eli is what he is. And maybe that's all he will ever be."

Despite the flood of criticism, Eli still had a job to do. The Giants were 7–4 and in the thick of the playoff race. The team rebounded with two wins on the road to move to 9–4. For some reason, the team seemed to play better on the road than at home. That trend continued in week 15, a home loss to Washington, and week 16, a road victory against the Buffalo Bills, their seventh road win in a row. Despite the team's success, Eli personally had done little to quiet his critics. In the four games following the Viking defeat, he threw more interceptions (4) than touchdowns (3), and his accuracy seemed to be getting worse.

In the Giants' 22–10 loss to the Washington Redskins on December 16, Eli completed just 18 of 52 passes. His 34 incomplete passes were the most in a game by any NFL quarterback in 40 years.

By the final game of the season, the Giants had clinched a playoff spot. Nothing was riding on week 17—except their pride. The team was hosting the New England Patriots, by far the NFL's best team at 15–0. Only the Giants stood between New England and the first perfect regular season since the 1972 Miami Dolphins. Many New York fans called for Coughlin to rest his starters, since the game meant so little to the Giants. But the coach still wasn't pleased with how his team was playing. Coughlin wanted to see the Giants finish strong. Trying to stop the Patriots from making history seemed like the perfect challenge. "I don't know any better way to be prepared for the playoffs than to go against a team that was 15–0," he said.

If the Patriots thought they'd have an easy march to 16–0, the Giants quickly changed their minds. On the offense's second play, Eli dropped back and heaved a long pass to Burress, who was sprinting downfield. The tall receiver leaped up and caught the ball for a 52-yard gain. A few plays later, Eli's 7-yard touch-down pass to Jacobs opened the scoring. He added a 3-yard pass to Kevin Boss at the end of the first half to give the Giants a 21–16 lead.

Eli came out firing in the second half. He looked calm and confident in the pocket. His accuracy problems seemed to be a thing of the past as he completed pass after pass. On New York's opening drive, he led the team to New England's 19-yard line. On a third-and-9 play, he took the snap from the shotgun and threw a strike to Burress on the right side of the field. Burress scored to extend the lead to 28–16. The Giants celebrated, feeling like they could be the team to stand in the way of New England.

But in the end, the Patriots were too much for the Giants. Early in the fourth quarter, New England took the lead in style, with a long 65-yard pass from Tom Brady to Randy Moss. The score gave Brady his fiftieth touchdown pass of the season, breaking Peyton's record of 49. It was Moss's twenty-third touchdown catch of the season, another record. Late in the game, Eli and Burress connected for one more touchdown, but it was too late. With a 38–35 win, the Patriots had their perfect regular season.

Despite the loss, the Giants felt good about their perform-ance. Eli had played his best game in a long time, completing 22 of 32 passes for 251 yards and 4 touchdowns. It was a much-needed boost of confidence. The big question remained: Could Eli and the Giants carry their momentum into the playoffs?

Chapter Nine

Super Surprise

The Giants were the NFC's number 5 seed out of six playoff teams. That meant that a home game in the playoffs was highly unlikely. Normally, that would be a bad thing. But for the Giants, the road seemed to be the perfect place to be. After all, they'd gone 7–1 on the road during the regular season compared to just 3–5 at home. So heading to Tampa Bay to face the Buccaneers in the first round didn't seem like such a tall task.

Tampa Bay would be Eli's third shot at a playoff win. But he knew it wasn't just about him. "My goals are the team goals," he said. "For me, it is just to go out there and play well and get a win . . . in the playoffs. . . . I think if the team does well, then that is the most important thing."

The game pitted two similar teams against each other. Like the Giants, the Bucs relied on a great defense to win games. They had one of the top pass defenses in the league, so many expected Eli to struggle. After all, he had been prone to interceptions all season, and no team was better suited than Tampa Bay to take advantage. The Bucs' plan was simple: Pressure Eli and force him to make bad decisions.

Despite holding Eli and the Giants without even a first down in the first quarter, the strategy didn't work. Eli made quick, good decisions throughout the game. He didn't do anything spectacular—in fact, only twice did he throw passes of more than 14 yards. But he kept making play after play, converting one first down after the next.

His dink-and-dunk approach aggravated the Tampa defenders. "He made little, annoying third-down conversions when he needed to," Bucs linebacker Barrett Ruud said. "If it is third and 8, he gets 8½ yards. That was frustrating."

Eli and the Giants held a 14–7 lead at halftime, and the Tampa frustration only grew as Eli led a pivotal second-half touchdown drive that ate up almost nine minutes. On the score, Eli used a pump fake (a fake pass in which the quarterback keeps the ball) to trick defensive back Ronde Barber, Tiki's brother, into leaving Toomer alone in the end zone. Eli capitalized on the mistake, hitting Toomer with a touchdown pass to seal the 24–14 win. It was the first playoff win of his career.

"Eli had a great game today," Toomer said. "He took what was out there and didn't force anything. He doesn't get real excited. There is more than one way to lead a team . . . and he showed that today."

The Giants didn't have much time to celebrate their victory. The next week, they had to travel to face the Cowboys again. Dallas—the NFC's top team at 13–3—had already beaten New York twice during the regular season, but Eli and his teammates were optimistic.

---

66 *I think as a team we seem to perform better on the road. I didn't know we won eight in a row. That's a great thing, because when it's the playoffs, if we're going to go as far as we want, we have to win every game on the road.* 99

—MICHAEL STRAHAN, FOLLOWING THE WIN OVER TAMPA BAY

"It's a tough challenge against Dallas, we know that," Eli said. "We played them two times; maybe the third will be the charm."

When Eli took the field in Dallas on January 13, he had already seen Peyton and the Colts lose to the Chargers. Any dreams Eli might have had of a Manning-Manning Super Bowl would have to wait. But it didn't detract from Eli's concentration. He had more than enough to worry about against the Cowboys.

The Giants started with a bang. On their opening possession, Eli connected with Toomer on a short pass. Two Dallas defenders badly missed the tackle, and Toomer jetted to the end zone for a 52-yard score and a 7–0 lead.

After that, Eli made his mark not by being spectacular but by being reliable. He took care of the ball, throwing no interceptions for the second game in a row. He completed short passes when he needed to. The game was physical and hard fought, exactly what New York wanted. And with 13 minutes to play, Jacobs burst through the line of scrimmage for a 1-yard touchdown and a 21–17 New York lead. From that point, it was all about the defense. The Cowboys put together three solid drives, but the Giants shut them down every time. When defensive back R.W. McQuarters intercepted a Tony Romo pass in the end zone with nine seconds to play, the game was over. Somehow, the Giants had done it! They had upset the mighty Cowboys and earned a trip to face the Green Bay Packers in the NFC Championship. After all his struggles during the regular season, Eli was one win away from the Super Bowl.

"I won't get tired of hearing that this week," Eli said. "No one's given us much credit and probably still won't. But that's okay. We like it that way."

---

66 *Everybody goes through their ups and downs and [Eli is] on the upswing right now. We're going to ride him as far as we can go.* **99**
—AMANI TOOMER ON ELI'S PLAYOFF IMPROVEMENT

Having won their last nine road games, the Giants faced yet another in the NFC Championship. But this one turned out to be like no other. The temperature in Green Bay plummeted while the wind kicked up. The Giants and Packers would be vying for a trip to the Super Bowl in one of the coldest games in recent memory, with the wind chill dipping to –24 degrees.

Eli's unemotional manner had often earned him criticism. But it was that same calm that helped the 27-year-old quarterback overcome a game filled with mistakes—dropped passes, missed field goals, and other lost opportunities. Despite the rash of mistakes, the Giants found themselves in a 20–20 tie with the heavily favored Packers early in the fourth quarter. With 12 minutes to play, Eli was hoping to lead the team to a go-ahead score. He was on his game again, completing short passes and handing off the ball to Ahmad Bradshaw, moving the Giants methodically down the field. He brought the Giants into field-goal range, but kicker Lawrence Tynes missed the 43-yard attempt, leaving the score tied.

The Giants didn't let the miss rattle them. With 2:15 to play, Eli had another chance. Once again, he drove the team deep into Green Bay territory. With just four seconds left, he spiked the ball to stop the clock. Tynes trotted out for a game-winning field-goal attempt. This time it was just a 36-yard kick—a virtual chip shot. But somehow, Tynes badly shanked the kick, and it sailed far to the left of the goal posts. The Giants players watched in disbelief as the Packer sideline and fans erupted. The game was headed to overtime.

Things looked even worse for New York when the Packers won the coin toss for the first possession. Veteran quarterback Brett Favre looked ready to engineer a game-winning drive. But on the second play of overtime, Favre badly missed receiver Donald Driver on a pass. Giants' cornerback Corey Webster was there for an interception, giving the Giants fantastic field position. Three plays later, Tynes had yet another attempt to win the game. This kick, however, was a 47-yarder, longer than either of his earlier misses. But Tynes didn't let this opportunity slip away. He booted the ball through the uprights. The Giants had done it! They were headed to the Super Bowl! The team stormed the field to celebrate with the kicker.

Eli tried to explain how the Giants had won three straight playoff games on the road. "It's just a matter of getting hot at the right time. It feels good because this is what you work for. We stuck with it, we believed in ourselves, and we got to the Super Bowl."

The Patriots were waiting. New England had upped its record to 18–0 with two playoff wins. In the two weeks leading up to the big game, most of the talk revolved around the Patriots. Were they the greatest team of all time? Was Brady the best quarterback the league had ever seen? At times, people talked about the Super Bowl almost as if it were the Patriots' coronation instead of a football game. To many, the Giants were just the team that the Pats would beat to complete their historic season. The question wasn't whether New England would win, but rather, by how much?

The Giants didn't buy it. Burress outright predicted a Giant victory. Eli was a bit more reserved. "We haven't been given a shot," he said, "but now we're here and I think we're deserving of it."

The challenge for Eli and the offense, according to experts, was to control the ball and keep Brady, Moss, and the powerful Patriot offense off the field. And that's exactly what they did in the game's first possession. If Eli was nervous, it didn't show. Once again, he looked sharp, though not spectacular, in leading the Giants on a long drive. Short passes and punishing runs highlighted a drive that took 16 plays, covered 63 yards, ate up almost 10 minutes, and resulted in a 32-yard Tynes field goal. At 9:59, it was the most time-consuming drive of any Super Bowl.

New England answered back with a touchdown on their first drive. Then the game became a defensive struggle. The New York defense was relentless, hurrying and hitting Brady on play after play. Neither team scored again in the first half, and both defenses put up zeros in the third quarter as well. That set the stage for one of the most memorable fourth quarters in Super Bowl history.

On the first play of the quarter, Eli saw tight end Kevin Boss open deep down the middle. He rifled a perfect pass, and Boss rumbled 45 yards to the New England 35-yard line. Three plays later, on third and 4, Eli found Steve Smith over the middle for 17 more yards. Then he gave New York a 10–7 lead with a perfect pass to Tyree in the end zone.

But the Patriots were undefeated for a reason. Brady led New England back with a long drive down the field and a 6-yard touchdown pass to Moss. With just 2:42 left, the Pats were back out front, 14–10.

Strangely, Eli felt good about being down four points. He and Peyton had talked about this exact situation. They'd agreed that having to go for the touchdown, knowing that playing it safe for a field goal wasn't an option, was a great motivator. "You like being down four when you know you have to score a touchdown to win the Super Bowl," Eli explained. "You can't write a better script."

NO JINXING IT

Peyton didn't attend Eli's victory in the NFC Championship game in Green Bay. He'd attended the Giants' embarrassing home loss to the Vikings and, according to Archie, Eli didn't want Peyton to bring him more bad luck. But Peyton was there for the Super Bowl, apparently without causing any ill effects!

The drive that followed will forever define Eli's career. From his own 17-yard line, Eli started off with an 11-yard strike to Toomer. Jacobs converted a big fourth-and-1 with 1:34 to play to keep the drive alive. After a 5-yard scramble and an incomplete pass, Eli and the Giants faced third and 5 from their own 44-yard line.

Then, on an amazing, improbable play, the Patriot defense charged as Eli took the snap. Several defenders broke through the Giants' protection. Defensive end Jarvis Green reached out to grab the scrambling quarterback as other defenders converged on Eli. It looked like a certain sack, which would have all but ended the Giants' hopes. But Eli ducked and twisted, somehow breaking free for a moment. He didn't waste that moment. He heaved a high-arcing desperation pass down the middle of the field toward Tyree. The wide receiver, sandwiched between defenders, leaped up for the high pass. He pinned the ball between an arm and the top of his helmet, somehow managing to hang on as he fell to the New England 24-yard line. The stunning play, which some later dubbed "the Great Escape," gave the Giants a first down and kept their hopes alive.

Eli still had work to do, however. He was sacked on the next play, then threw an incomplete pass on second down. Just like that, the Giants were in a bad situation again—this time third and 11. But once again, Eli came through in the clutch, hitting Smith near the sideline for 12 yards.

Just 39 seconds remained. Eli knew the Pats would be coming hard. So he took the snap and looked quickly for his favorite target—Burress. The receiver shook his defender, and Eli threw a high, soft pass toward the left corner of the end zone. Burress grabbed it in stride—touchdown! The stadium erupted and the Giants celebrated.

Brady and the Patriots came onto the field with 29 seconds to engineer a winning or tying drive. The New England quarterback heaved a long pass toward Jabar Gaffney, but it fell incomplete. On second down, the Giants sacked Brady, forcing the Patriots into third and 20. On the next two plays, Brady looked deep for Moss, but the two couldn't connect. The Giants took over possession with just one second to play. Eli took a final snap, dropped to one knee, and the celebration began. Shocking almost everyone—except themselves—the Giants had done it! They'd beaten the undefeated Patriots and, in one of the biggest upsets in NFL history, had become the Super Bowl champions.

Eli completed 19 of 34 passes in the game for 255 yards and 2 touchdowns. For his fourth-quarter heroics, he was named the game's MVP—just a year after Peyton had won the award.

Eli's prize for winning the Super Bowl MVP award was his choice of any 2009 model of Cadillac. Eli picked an Escalade Hybrid—a fuel-conscious sport utility vehicle (SUV).

"The guys on this team and the run we've made, it's hard to believe—it really is," Eli said. "The drive at the end, there were so many clutch plays by so many guys. It is an unbelievable game and an unbelievable feeling."

Eli hoisted the Lombardi Trophy, awarded each year to the Super Bowl's winning team. He was no longer simply Peyton's little brother in the eyes of the football world. Eli was a Super Bowl champion.

Being His Own Manning

For Giants fans, Eli Manning brings a mix of excitement and frustration. As he showed in New York's remarkable playoff run and Super Bowl victory, he has enormous talent. He is calm, intelligent, and athletically gifted. But as much of the 2007 regular season showed, he's also wildly inconsistent. He can look like one of the league's best quarterbacks one game and a guy who is about to be cut from the league in the next. His decision making often seems flawed—a big part of the reason that his interception numbers are still high for an NFL starter. Yet when he's on, it's impossible to deny that he's tough to beat.

Even with Eli's Super Bowl win and MVP trophy, people will probably never stop comparing him to his brother. Fans watch Peyton play with intense emotion and wonder why Eli isn't the same way. Many fans still expect Eli to be a younger version of Peyton. But that's never going to happen. They may be brothers, but they're very different quarterbacks and, more important, very different people. "Easy" Eli doesn't rant and rave and shout at his teammates in hopes of getting them pumped up. That's not his style, and it never has been. He doesn't seek attention the way his brother often seems to. When he's active in a charity, such as raising money for the children's hospital at the University of Mississippi, he does it with as little fanfare as possible. While Peyton endorses dozens of products in commercials, Eli endorses only a few, preferring to stay in the background. Even his wedding with Abby, on April 19, 2008, was modest compared to most celebrity weddings. Eli doesn't make headlines off the field—he's content to just play football.

What will the future hold for Eli? Will he be able to capitalize on his Super Bowl heroics and become the quarterback the Giants envisioned when they traded for him in 2004? Or will he continue to struggle with his accuracy and interception ratio? Coming off one of the biggest Super Bowl upsets in history, the spotlight will be brighter than ever. But Eli should be used to that. His football career has been scrutinized almost since the day he picked up a ball.

PERSONAL STATISTICS

Name:

Elisha Nelson Manning

Nicknames:

Easy

Born:

January 3, 1981, New Orleans, Louisiana

College:

University of Mississippi (Ole Miss)

Height:

6' 4"

Weight:

225 lbs.

Throws:

Right-handed

COLLEGE STATISTICS

Year	Team	Games	Att	Comp	Yards	TD	Int
2000	MISS	6	33	16	170	0	1
2001	MISS	11	408	259	2,948	31	9
2002	MISS	13	481	279	3,401	21	15
2003	MISS	13	441	275	3,600	29	10
Career		43	1,363	829	10,119	81	35

Key: Att: attempts; Comp: completions; TD: touchdowns; Int: interceptions

REGULAR-SEASON STATISTICS

Year	Team	Games	Att	Comp	Yards	TD	Int
2004	NYG	9	197	95	1,043	6	9
2005	NYG	16	557	294	3,762	24	17
2006	NYG	16	522	301	3,244	24	18
2007	NYG	16	529	297	3,336	23	20
Career		57	1,805	987	11,385	77	64

Key: Att: attempts; Comp: completions; TD: touchdowns; Int: interceptions

GLOSSARY

audible: a change of the play called by the quarterback at the line of scrimmage

blitz: a defensive play in which defenders who don't usually rush the quarterback do so

draft: a system for selecting new players for professional sports teams

endorse: to promote a product in advertisements

incentive: a part of a contract that calls for additional money to be paid for certain achievements, such as a specific number of touchdown passes in a season or a high passer rating

line of scrimmage: the line on which the ball is placed at the beginning of a play and where the linemen on both sides of the ball battle for position

pocket: the protected area behind a team's offensive line, in which the quarterback usually operates

redshirt: to not play a college player in the freshman year. The player can practice with his or her team and doesn't lose a year of college eligibility.

rookie: a first-year player

scholarship: money given to a student to help pay the costs of schooling

SOURCES

3   Steven Godfrey, "Rebel Run Culminates with Cotton Bowl Victory," *Daily Mississippian*, January 7, 2004. http://media.www .thedmonline.com/media/storage/ paper876/news/2004/01/07/ Sports/Rebel.Run.Culminates.With. Cotton.Bowl.Victory-1587997.shtml (April 28, 2008).

5   Archie and Peyton Manning, *Manning* (New York: HarperEntertainment, 2000), 177.

6   Karen Crouse, "Eli Manning Took Cues from Mother," *New York Times*, January 29, 2008, http://www .nytimes.com/2008/01/29/sports/ football/29manning.html?em&ex =1201842000&en=e28086730389da c0&ei=5087 (April 3, 2008).

6   Manning, 167.

7   Crouse, "Eli Manning Took Cues from Mother."

9   Manning, 238.

9   Ray Glier, "Manning Keeps Heisman Hype on the Field," *New York Times*, July 31, 2003, http://query .nytimes.com/gst/fullpage.html ?res=990DE4D8143EF932A05754C0 A9659C8B63 (April 28, 2008).

10 Manning, 315.

12 Clay Chandler, "Manning Nears Close of His Career," *Daily Mississippian*, November 20, 2003, http://media.www.thedmonline .com/media/storage/paper876/ news/2003/11/20/Sports/Manning .Nears.Close.Of.His.Career- 1587837.shtml (April 28, 2008).

13 Ibid.

14 AP, "Ole Miss' Mellow Manning Right at Home in Oxford," *NCAAsports.com*, n.d., http://www .ncaasports.com/football/mens/ story/6570792 (March 10, 2008).

15 Peter Ross, "Eli Manning: A Golden Arm and a Sterling Pedigree," *Daily Mississippian*, August 31, 2001, http://media.www.thedmonline .com/media/storage/paper876/ news/2001/08/31/Undefined Section/Eli-Manning.A.Golden.Arm .And.A.Sterling.Pedigree- 1580154.shtml (April 28, 2008).

16 Tom Dienhart, "Another Manning Charts His Own Path at Ole Miss," *Sportingnews.com*, March 26, 2001, http://findarticles.com/p/articles/ mi_m1208/is_13_225/ai_72609777 (April 28, 2008).

16–17 Dienhart, "Another Manning Charts His Own Path."

17 Ross, "Eli Manning: A Golden Arm and a Sterling Pedigree."

18 Ibid.

19 Peter Ross, "Rebs Roll," *Daily Mississippian*, October 15, 2001, http://media.www.thedmonline .com/media/storage/paper876/ news/2001/10/15/Sports/Rebs- Roll-1580718.shtml (April 28, 2008).

20 Clay Chandler, "Rebels Storm Death Valley, Get Crucial SEC Win," *Daily Mississippian*, October 29, 2001, http://media.www.thedmonline .com/media/storage/paper876/ news/2001/10/29/Sports/Geaux .To.Hell.Lsu-1580865.shtml (April 28, 2008).

24 Kyle Veazey, "No Bones About It— Florida Is a Marked Foe," *Daily Mississippian*, October 3, 2002, http://media.www.thedmonline .com/media/storage/paper876/ news/2002/10/03/Sports/No .Bones.About.It.Florida.Is.A.Marked .Foe-1583729.shtml (April 7, 2008).

26 Kyle Veazey, "Eli's Big Decision Will Wait Until After Bowl," *Daily Mississippian*, December 3, 2002, http://media.www.thedmonline .com/media/storage/paper876/ news/2002/12/03/Sports/Elis-Big .Decision.Will.Wait.Until.After.Bowl- 1584346.shtml (April 28, 2008).

27 Ibid.

27 Joe Drape, "Eli Rewrites Manning Legacy at Ole Miss," *New York Times*, November 22, 2003, http://query.nytimes.com/gst/fullpage.html?res=9C0CE6DA133BF931A15752C1A9659C8B63 (April 7, 2008).

28 "Nebraska vs. Ole Miss," *USA Today*, December 28, 2002, http://www.usatoday.com/sports/scores102/102361/20021227NCAAFOLEMISS—0.htm#RCPS (April 28, 2008).

29 Kyle Veazey, "Eli Offers a Simple Explanation: I Wanted to Stay," *Daily Mississippian*, January 17, 2003, http://media.www.thedmonline.com/media/storage/paper876/news/2003/01/17/Sports/Eli-Offers.A.Simple.Explanation.i.Wanted.To.Stay-1584570.shtml (April 28, 2008).

31 Jay Glier, "Manning Keeps Heisman Hype on Field," *New York Times*, July 31, 2003, http://query.nytimes.com/gst/fullpage.html?res=990DE4D8143EF932A05754C0A9659C8B63&scp=4&sq=Eli+Manning+Newman&st=nyt (April 28, 2008).

31 Amanda Vierck, "Manning Returns to Lead Ole Miss into Battle," *Daily Reveille*, September 12, 2003, http://media.www.lsureveille.com/media/storage/paper868/news/2003/09/12/Features/Manning.Returns.To.Lead.Ole.Miss.Into.Battle-2046879.shtml (April 28, 2008).

33 Steven Godfrey, "For One More Year, Eli Manning Lives Under the Microscope," *Daily Mississipian*, September 12, 2003, http://www.thedmonline.com/media/storage/paper876/news/2003/09/12/UndefinedSection/For-One.More.Year.Eli.Manning.Lives.Under.The.Microscope-1586668.shtml (April 28, 2008).

34 AP, "Rebels Need a Repeat of Alabama Performance against Arkansas," *ESPN.com*, October 20, 2003, http://sports.espn.go.com/espn/wire?id=1642705 (April 28, 2008).

35 AP, "Obomanu Stars, Then Drops Winning TD," *ESPN.com*, November 8, 2003, http://sports.espn.go.com/ncf/recap?gameId=233120002 (April 28, 2008).

36 Josh Wilbert, "Manning Slips in Heroic Attempt," *Daily Mississipian*, November 24, 2003, http://www.thedmonline.com/media/storage/paper876/news/2003/11/24/Sports/Manning.Slips.In.Heroic.Attempt-1587888.shtml (April 28, 2008).

37 Josh Wilbert, "Manning Slips in Heroic Attempt."

39 Godfrey, "Rebel Run Culminates with Cotton Bowl Victory."

42 Lynn Zinser, "Manning's Day Gets Miles Better After a Trade to the Giants," *New York Times*, April 25, 2004, http://query.nytimes.com/gst/fullpage.html?res=9405EFD9133AF936A15757C0A9629C8B63 (April 28, 2008).

42–43 Ibid.

43 Ibid.

43–44 Lynn Zinser, "Manning's Fast Signing Is a Bonus All Around," *New York Times*, July 30, 2004, http://query.nytimes.com/gst/fullpage.html?res=9502E1D7113DF933A05754C0A9629C8B63 (April 18, 2008).

45 Ibid.

47 Lynn Zinser, "Present Imperfect, Future Is Manning," *New York Times*, November 22, 2004, http://www.nytimes.com/2004/11/22/sports/football/22giants.html (April 18, 2008).

48 Ibid.

48 Jeff Zillgitt, "Giants' Manning Licks His Wounds," *USA Today*, December 12, 2004, http://www.usatoday.com/sports/columnist/zillgitt/2004-12-12-zillgitt_x.htm (April 18, 2008).

49 Lynn Zinser, "Reason to Cheer Amid a Chorus of Doubts," *New York Times*, December 19, 2004, http://www.nytimes.com/2004/12/19/sports/football/19giants.html (April 18, 2008).

51 Tom Canavan, "Barber's Milestone Gives Giants 28–24 Win vs. Dallas," *USA Today*, January 3, 2005, http://www.usatoday.com/sports/football/games/2005-01-03-giants-cowboys_x.htm (April 18, 2008).

53 Lee Jenkins, "Running, Catching, Throwing, Tomlinson Overwhelms Giants," *New York Times*, September 26, 2005, http://www.nytimes.com/2005/09/26/sports/football/26giants.html (April 18, 2008).

54 Judy Battista, "Manning's Learning Curve Loses Its Arc," *New York Times*, October 3, 2005, http://www.nytimes.com/2005/10/03/sports/football/03giants.html (April 18, 2008).

57 John Branch, "Manning's Career Could Use an Off-Season Exorcism," *New York Times*, January 11, 2006, http://www.nytimes.com/2006/01/11/sports/football/11giants.html (April 18, 2008).

58 David Picker, "In Panthers, Hobbled Giants Face a Rugged Test," *New York Times*, January 2, 2006, http://query.nytimes.com/gst/fullpage.html?res=9F06E6D61030F931A35752C0A9609C8B63 (April 18, 2008).

59 Mark Maske, "Panthers Roll in a Giant Way," *Washington Post*, January 29, 2006, http://www.washingtonpost.com/wp-dyn/content/article/2006/01/08/AR2006010800574.html (April 18, 2008).

60 John Branch, "No Chance, No Mercy," *New York Times*, January 9, 2006, http://www.nytimes.com/2006/01/09/sports/football/09giants.html (April 18, 2008).

61 Warren St. John, "The Brother Bowl," *New York Times*, August 20, 2006, http://www.nytimes.com/2006/08/20/sports/playmagazine/20manning.html (April 18, 2008).

62 Michael Eisen, "Archie Shares Thoughts on Manning Bowl," *Giants.com*, May 12, 2006, http://www.giants.com/news/eisen/story.asp?story_id=15577 (April 18, 2008).

62 AP, "Where's the Brotherly Love? Peyton, Colts Nip Eli, Giants," *ESPN.com*, September 10, 2006, http://sports.espn.go.com/nfl/recap?gameId=260910019 (April 18, 2008).

63 Ibid.

65 John Branch, "Manning Doesn't Lose His Cool During the Giants' Comeback," *New York Times*, September 19, 2006, http://www.nytimes.com/2006/09/19/sports/football/19giants.html (April 18, 2008).

66 AP, "Jaguars Contain Tiki, Confuse Eli in Win Over Giants," *ESPN.com*, November 20, 2006, http://sports.espn.go.com/nfl/recap?gameId=261120030 (April 18, 2008).

66 John Branch, "An Erratic Manning Puts the Giants on Blue Alert," *New York Times*, November 26, 2006, http://www.nytimes.com/2006/11/26/sports/football/26giants.html (April 18, 2008).

67 AP, "Young Rallies Titans from 21-point Deficit to Stun Giants," *ESPN.com*, November 26, 2006, http://sports.espn.go.com/nfl/recap?gameId=261126010 (April 18, 2008).

68 AP, "Young Rallies Titans from 21-point Deficit to Stun Giants."

68–69 Tom Canavan, "Saints 30, Giants 7," *Yahoo! Sports*, December 24, 2006, http://sports.yahoo.com/nfl/recap?gid=20061224019 (April 18, 2008).

71 John Branch, "A Franchise in Flux, a Quarterback at a Standstill," *New York Times*, January 7, 2007, http://www.nytimes.com/2007/01/07/sports/football/07giants.html (April 18, 2008).

73 Michael Eisen, "Manning to Marry," *Giants.com*, March 22, 2007, http://www.giants.com/news/eisen/story.asp?story_id=24384 (April 18, 2008).

77 John Branch, "Rough Day for Manning and the Giants," *New York Times*, November 26, 2007, http://www.nytimes.com/2007/11/26/sports/football/26giants.html (April 18, 2008).

78 John Branch, "Third-and-Ready?" *New York Times*, September 3, 2006, http://query.nytimes.com/gst/fullpage.html?res=9405E0DB1F3EF930A3575AC0A9609C8B63 (April 18, 2008).

78 Don Banks, "Snap Judgments: Manning's Mediocrity, Gibbs' Gaffe, Garrard's Growth," *SI.com*, November 25, 2007, http://sportsillustrated.cnn.com/2007/writers/don_banks/11/25/snap.judgments/ (April 18, 2008).

79–80 AP, "Pats' Year of Perfection Capped by Thrilling Comeback Win over Giants," *ESPN.com*, December 29, 2007, http://sports.espn.go.com/nfl/recap?gameId=271229019 (April 18, 2008).

77 Tom Pedulla, "Giants, Eli Look for Answers after Humbling Loss," *USA Today*, November 25, 2007, http://www.usatoday.com/sports/football/nfl/2007-11-25-vikings-giants_N.htm (April 28, 2008).

82 AP, "Eli Manning Looking for First Postseason Win," *Sportingnews.com*, January 1, 2008, http://www.sportingnews.com/yourturn/viewtopic.php?t=332006 (April 18, 2008).

83 AP, "Giants March on After Beating Host Buccaneers," *NFL.com*, January 6, 2008, http://www.nfl.com/gamecenter/recap?game_id=29518 (April 28, 2008).

83–84 AP, "Giants March on After Beating Host Buccaneers."

84 AP, "First Stop Tampa, Next Stop, Texas," *SI.com*, January 6, 2008, http://sportsillustrated.cnn.com/football/nfl/scoreboards/2008/01/06/2815_viewcast_recap.html (April 28, 2008).

84 AP, "Giants March on After Beating Host Buccaneers."

85 AP, "Eli Manning Looking for First Postseason Win."

86 Jamie Aron, "Cowboys Crumble in Playoffs Again; Giants Headed to Green Bay," *Yahoo! Sports*, January 13, 2008, http://sports.yahoo.com/nfl/recap;_ylt=AgcVps.me4_6PLqUVNMzRdL.uLYF?gid=20080113006 (April 28, 2008).

86 AP, "Cowboys Fall Short on Last Effort as Giants Move on to Face Packers," *ESPN.com*, January 13, 2008, http://scores.espn.go.com/nfl/recap?gameId=280113006 (April 28, 2008).

88 AP, "Manning, Giants Head to Super Bowl for Rematch with Pats," *ESPN.com.*, January 20, 2008, http://sports.espn.go.com/nfl/recap?gameId=280120009 (April 28, 2008).

88 Ibid.

90 Ralph Vacchiano, "Giants Stuff Patriots to Win Super Bowl," *New York Daily News*, February 5, 2008, http://www.nydailynews.com/sports/football/giants/2008/02/03/2008-02-03_giants_stun_patriots_to_win_super_bowl-2.html (April 28, 2008).

93 Greg Garber, "Eli, Monster Defense Power Giants to Shocking Super Bowl Victory," *ESPN.com.*, February 3, 2008, http://sports.espn.go.com/nfl/recap?gameId=280203017 (April 28, 2008).

BIBLIOGRAPHY

Chandler, Clay. "Manning Nears Close of His Career." *Daily Mississippian*. November 20, 2003. http://media.www .thedmonline.com/media/storage/paper876/news/ 2003/11/20/Sports/Manning.Nears.Close.Of.His .Career-1587837.shtml (April 28, 2008).

Crouse, Karen. "Eli Manning Took Cues from Mother." *New York Times*. January 29, 2008. http://www.nytimes.com/ 2008/01/29/sports/football/29manning.html?em&ex =1201842000&en=e28086730389dac0&ei=5087 (April 3, 2008).

Manning, Archie and Peyton. *Manning*. New York: HarperEntertainment, 2000.

St. John, Warren. "The Brother Bowl." *New York Times*. August 20, 2006. http://www.nytimes.com/2006/08/ 20/sports/playmagazine/20manning.html (April 18, 2008).

WEBSITES

Giants.com

http://www.giants.com

The official home page of the New York Giants includes all the latest team news and statistics, with photos, videos, and more.

ESPN.com—Eli Manning

http://sports.espn.go.com/nfl/players/profile?statsId=6760

ESPN.com's player page on Eli includes career statistics, feature articles, and a game log.

NFL.com—The Official Site of the National Football League

http://www.nfl.com

The NFL's official site includes scores, news, statistics, video features, and other information for football fans.

OleMissSports.com

http://www.olemisssports.com/

Read all about the Ole Miss Rebels football team at the official site of the University of Mississippi Athletics.

INDEX